CONFESSIONS OF A PRISON COOK

A FUSION OF FOOD AND CRIME

ERIKA SOMERFELD AND PHILIP LONGO

D1595760

Waterside Productions

Printed in the United States of America

First Printing, 2021

ISBN-13: 978-1-954968-84-4 print edition
ISBN-13: 978-1-954968-85-1 ebook edition

Waterside Productions
2055 Oxford Ave
Cardiff, CA 92007
www.waterside.com

TABLE OF CONTENTS

"WE HAD ROAST BEEF FOR DINNER TONIGHT . . .
NO MOM, IT'S *NOT* BETTER THAN YOURS!"

PART I
PRE-HEAT

CHAPTER 1

OUT OF THE FRYING PAN, INTO THE MIRE

Give them great meals of beef and iron and steel,
they will eat like wolves and fight like devils.
—William Shakespeare

The Billiard Club was born in Chelsea, New York in 1988. Floor-to-ceiling glass windows twenty feet high, an antique wood bar the width of the room, chandeliers that highlighted red velvet draping, and Greek faux-marble columns. This gaudy, gorgeous place was the city's new hot spot.

Woody Allen, Denzel Washington, Whitney Houston, George Michael, Christina Applegate, and Matt Dillon frequented the club. Eddie Murphy's hit *Boomerang* filmed here, and all the guys especially enjoyed the high fashion model shoots. We never had to advertise; success came word-of-mouth. Every TV station in Manhattan covered our joint, and we soon opened franchises in Atlanta, Philly, and Long Island.

The club became home to a group of Asian high school kids whose education extended to playing pool and darts all day. They'd invite me to join in Thirteen Card Chinese Poker, even letting me win once in a while. They'd snort coke and smoke weed, which I allowed. Drinking champagne upstairs with twin sisters was the highest I got.

I met Howie at the Billiard Club in 1989. He used to deliver gambling machines for our joint, owned by … waste management executives. The clown was short, rotund, and sported a red beard. He taught me the ropes of low-level fraud, and I began charging pool cues on credit cards he'd stolen for $150 bucks a shot. He also invited me to middle-of-the-night, VIP warehouse sales, where everything was marked down to zero.

Howie said the Orientals could be a source for heroin and a princely paycheck. Seeing the glass as half full of money, greed led me to mention it to gang leader Wen Li, who got back to me two years later. It all felt so damn exciting; the buzz was blocking my brain.

I didn't see myself as a drug conspirator, rather as a middle-aged middleman hooking up a buyer and seller on a silver platter. I believed the deal could elevate my status to Big Shot. Maybe I'd get tight with platinum model Sherry, instead of being her polite pal, Phil.

So I was off to Queens now, to meet a dozen armed Chinese teens. They didn't speak English, but aptly communicated that I needed to buy on the spot. With Wen Li translating, I left alive, carrying a sample big enough to divide five ways. I walked it over to some Sicilians who worked at Nell's nightclub nearby. They made it crystal clear that the H was weak, and I'd be too, if I didn't circle back with better stuff.

The second sample was another turkey. By now I was keen to forget the whole thing. But Wen Li arranged a third meeting and, ever ignorant, I agreed. Howie's contacts loved the goods and agreed to $1.2M. Our piece of the pie would be $250,000 by Sunday night, but I was obsessed with eyeballing the money before the deal went down.

Knowing I wouldn't sleep, I called the client. Within an hour, three guys with machine guns kept me wide awake while I ran the cash through a pair of electric counters. No threats of killing my family, no horse heads in my bed. The threesome even ordered room service.

Wen Li was packing powder when we met in the hotel lobby later that afternoon. We headed upstairs with his boy-bodyguard to meet the mobsters, while Howie sat solo at the bar. I felt pretty gangsta' going to make the deal, especially when six DEA agents with laser rifles answered the door and belted out a chorus of *Get Your Fucking Hands Up!*

Wen Li was stripped of the smack, and I was body searched for guns. Reality hadn't stuck a fork in me yet, so I yapped, "The only weapon I have is a six-inch dick." I was tossed to the ground like a sack of sausage. A second agent swiped the bodyguard's unloaded weapon, while the other walloped him across the face, cracking, "Before you do a job, fuck for brains, load your gun and take a shit, kid." The youngster took his advice and crapped himself on the spot.

Howie fucking Fuchs set me up. After pleading guilty to drug charges, he became a snitch for the DEA. His sentence was 40 to Life, but he only served seven, forever branding him my 'Seven Year Bitch.' I'd spend two years in New York's Otisville Federal Prison with 1,500 men, and another 2,500 days inside the minimum-security "Camp" with 99 other nonviolent cons.

This memoir is a smorgasbord of my time served, the foods I served up, and the crime that never served me. I've changed some names to protect the Sinnocent.

CHAPTER 2

CANNED

I ended up spending twenty-five hours behind bars.
I had a terrific egg sandwich.
—Shia LaBeouf

Otisville penitentiary looms atop a mountain surrounded by a ring of roads that look like a noose. Newbies were called "fish," and that felt on scale, since I had been sent upstream and was surely going to drown. My cellmate and I shared a sink, a steel door, a metal toilet and a tiny common window. This is where I first laid eyes on The Mole.

Jesus was a striking mix of beauty and beast. A strawberry birthmark planted between his eyes topped off his anchor-shaped nose and sky-high cheekbones. You couldn't help but stare at the Mexican mutt. The most inked up, ghetto guys stepped aside when he passed. Christ, he looked like trouble.

The first thing you get as an inmate is the blues. Then it's prison greens, a pathetically hard pillow, and a used army blanket. Second course: a kid-sized soap, toothbrush and toothpaste. If your hair was long, you'd have to hit the brig barbershop. Mine was fluffy and frizzy. On a good day I looked like Ralph Lauren; on a bad one, Einstein.

Putting on my laceless Bobos (state-issued footwear with as much support as Dad's cardboard-insoled shoes), I eyed a guy no more than five feet tall. He asked if I wanted anything from the commissary. Pass.

I didn't want to be indebted to anyone, especially day one of my ten-year sentence.

No matter. The little dude was determined to teach me big house etiquette. He dropped a netted laundry bag full of sweets at my feet hours later, and taught me slammer-slang when he suggested I "Ration the Wham Whams." Then, he plopped down two packs of ramen noodles (aka prison cash), canned tuna, and some decent sneakers.

Surprised and relieved, I said thanks as he disappeared into the steel sunset. This generous guy turned out to be a killer little shrimp. He'd been indicted for twenty murders as an assassin.

CHAPTER 3

MISTEAKS

Failure is the condiment that gives success its flavor.
—Truman Capote

A gang of cockroaches invaded my lockless locker, which reminded me of an episode that went down prior to my '92 arrest. My apartment in Manhattan was broken into and trashed by the DEA after an erroneous rumor that I was dealing cocaine. The informant had to be Barry, my former Billiard Club partner who had a grudge-shaped cue up his ass 'cause I put him out for stealing. Barry's now serving ten-to-life for knocking over a Florida market.

The agents found "roach cookies" hidden in plain sight in my living room. The little white bandits were just bacon grease, boric acid, flour, and water sculpted into snowy-looking meatballs to keep cockroaches at bay. The agent's embarrassment triggered them to trash my fridge, pulverize my silk rug and slash every painting and piece of furniture. Cherry on top: the cookie monsters treated themselves to $33,000 in legit cash stashed in my freezer inside an empty tub of mint ice cream.

I thought my prison days might not be so dreary when I caught sight of a mouthwatering blonde filling up my window view. Nurse Blackie had ruby lips, sapphire eyes, and a uniform that was a size too tight. What a gem – like a sparkling butterfly in a dirty garage. Men howled, but she just bimbled through their wolf whistles.

I was always a man who preferred blondes, but when I met a quiet brunette named Sheila in 1960, with small blue eyes and a grand Irish figure, I knew she would become my wife. (I didn't know it would be after a year of sexless dating.) Sheila wore little makeup, and her boyish, short hair framed the tiny pearl earrings she wore every day. My wife also worked full-time, so we mostly watched TV together and tended to our acre in Freehold, New Jersey.

My spouse came from a solidly dysfunctional family whose members included Alcoholism, Mental Illness, and Racism. (They hated that I was Italian; was it because Sheila's aunt hung herself after becoming pregnant by a Wop?) I felt sorry for the dad. Arthritis left his hands and legs gnarled, and psoriasis scarred his face with beet red patches. He had utter disdain for life and the people in it. When we went to her apartment after the ceremony where he was a no-show, he tossed my bride's belongings out a four-story window. Her nightgown in the filthy gutter was a sign of times to come.

I was released on $500,000 bail before I was sentenced. The money was put up by my brother-in-law, my sister (who jeopardized her pension), and two friends who furnished collateral. Sheila refused to contribute her half of our home. I don't blame her. Despite the fact we had been together for thirty years, I was a self-centered asshole for twenty-nine and a half of them.

I took care of her financially, but was an ambitious, immature husband. The bit of passion we once had faded into the shadows of daily life, and we mentally and physically went our separate ways. We had a child to fit in, but more so to have someone to love, and someone to love us. My well-adapted, bright daughter remains my North Star.

After doing time at Fordham Law School, I nabbed a degree in finance and fastened to a job at a top bank in New York. Within months, I was promoted to Vice President. I worked there for a decade, during which time my father died. I soon bonded with a much older client, Scott, who introduced me to The Good Life. We partied with fashion's elite, like Giorgio Armani and Carolina Herrera, and yachted to private islands while devouring aged steaks and even older French wine.

The lifestyle upgrade made me cocky doodle dumb. The inevitable, ethical violation I committed on Scott's behalf got me axed from the bank, with execs spreading shit that clients paid me to let them overborrow. I soon ended up in a soulless job as a footman in a hock shop. Over the next three years my salary, marriage, and confidence tanked.

Thinking about my wreckage got me down, but Nurse Blackie circling back around kept me up. I hoped she was the gift that'd keep on giving at Otisville.

CHAPTER 4

DINNER THEATER

Money won is twice as sweet as money earned.
—Paul Newman

Cons flipping cards on the cement flashed me back to running a poker game above the movie house where I worked as a teen. My parents made it clear that cinema and restaurants were luxuries for others, so I got busy. At ten, I was scoring a quarter for every supermarket delivery, and at thirteen I set pins at a bowling alley. An Assistant Manager job at a Coney Island theater was my nineteenth birthday present.

My boss there would retrieve torn ticket stubs off the ground, mark them as refunds, and pocket the cash. I started to copycat the dog, and actually fed myself off that RKO floor for months. (Clearly I had a natural, entrepreneurial spirit. Six years earlier, I stole my Boy Scout leader's *Playboys* from his john and sold them for a voluminous profit.)

I began holding a game above the once-Vaudevillian playhouse every Saturday night. Cloudy, oval mirrors were still backstage in the hoary dressing rooms. Pals didn't rank next to the hunnies and the money, but I invited a few guys to play anyway. People watched flicks below as we jockeyed for an inside straight. Soundtracks to *Journey to the Center of the Earth* and *Pillow Talk* scored our games, along with the constant clunking sound of the vending machine dropping Bit-O-Honeys, Mounds, and O! Henry bars.

The Blue Grotto was a dive next door. Nathan's hot dogs and their crinkle-cut fries up the street were my obsession, but I cooked up a deal with Anthony from the Grotto: I ate gratis, and he saw movies for free. I usually inhaled pizza and slurped warm Rheingold beer during hands. Popcorn was banned from theaters at the time – picture shows were once fancy affairs – but I let customers sneak it in. I didn't care, there was poker to play.

With no kings or queens in sight, one night I jacked up the action. The minute the second show ended, I flicked the main theater lights on and off, faster and faster, signaling the crowd to scram – get out! But an elderly lady was injured peeling down a flight of stairs, and I got canned the next day. Maybe it was being browbeat as "Silly Philly" when I was a little crumb grinder, but I didn't feel so pea-brained now, learning the ways of the world.

My original aspiration of joining the Air Force took a dive, despite passing the pilot officer's qualifying test. That plan could have offered me more stability, but it would have been bland in comparison to life in the fast lane.

"Can't you do something with that besides
caramelize your crème brûlée?"

PART 2
SIMMERING

CHAPTER 5

RIN TIN TIN FOILED

If your mother cooks Italian food, why go to a restaurant?
—Martin Scorsese

Saturdays meant riding the trolley with my family from Brooklyn to Coney Island. There was never extra money to buy ice cream or hot dogs, but mom made egg and tuna salad sandwiches. The sun caused the juice from the tuna to soak the bread, making it tastier. Any meal bound us all together; cooking in my Brooklyn house was the glue.

Mom gave her homey meals names like "Penne à la Paul" for my brother, and "Apples Anita" for my sister. "Potatoes Philip" was named for me, and for dad, "Beef Burgundy Benjamin," which was really just chuck steak with A1 Sauce. Anytime I make her signature dish, which us kids named "Gilda's Lasagna," I feel connected to all four feet, ten inches of her. I can see her in front of me, her dress pinned with a gold antique brooch like a matron from a former generation.

Gilda visited in 1993, my first year inside. On duty that day was part-time paralegal, Greta, and godly southern guard, Grayson. His pale green eyes and mouth full of gold teeth were an astonishing contrast to his black, pigmented skin. When I was moved to the minimum-security Camp two years later, I prepared all his meals, and he usually complimented my cooking. I knew feeding the guards well was good business, but I also sympathized with Grayson for all the shit the inmates dished out, especially Jesus.

Mama had cooked lasagna that day. She smuggled it into the slammer, having stuffed it deep inside her girdle, double-wrapped in foil. This wasn't murder mystery dinner theater: she meant business. But bad things always happened when Greta was on duty. She was an overeater with a nasty attitude who spawned from military school. I would hate to be the son of that bitch.

Greta's German Shepherd companion, Fury, made her debut at Otisville by sniffing mom's backside over and going mutt-wild from the spicy aroma. The dog toppled her, ripping the front of her gray dress and tangling her silver hair. When red sauce-covered noodles spilled out, everyone in the room gasped, thinking an old lady's bloody guts were pouring out. Fury, paw-high in marinara sauce, wavered between eating the pasta or my parent. Having the dogs attack you in jail was the mother of all punishments.

Grayson used scripture to calm Mom down post strip search, but she was tough. Being denied visitation for six months is what worried her. I heard Greta had a rare moment of decency when she helped mother dress. That's what it took to move this rock of resentment: an old woman attacked by dogs.

Grayson tried to sugarcoat the news that I'd have no visitors for months by quoting the Bible ("The Lord likes the brokenhearted"), but his teeth distracted me: he had more gold in them than Mike Tyson. Would I ever stop putting my family through hell? I wasn't often told "I love you," but I don't recall being called a moron, either.

I didn't talk to anyone about what happened; keeping your cool in the cooler was a must.

RECIPE: SHEPHERD LASAGNA

4 cloves of black garlic
3 cans (14.5 oz.) diced tomatoes
2 packages lasagna pasta
2 large thinly sliced baking potatoes
1 lb. of ground beef
1 can of drained peas
1 onion
1 lb. of ricotta
12 oz. sliced mozzarella
½ cup grated parmesan cheese
¼ cup olive oil
¼ cup chopped basil
1 tbsp. oregano

Heat the oven to 325°F. Brown beef in a tablespoon of olive oil and set in a large pot. Sauté black garlic in olive oil and add sliced onion. Simmer on low until the onion loses its color. Add tomatoes, oregano, and basil. Let simmer for 2 hours. Stir occasionally and remove from heat.

Boil packages of pasta, one at a time, in a large pot of salted water with a tablespoon of olive oil. Cook for 8 minutes to create al dente noodles. Drain and place the individual pieces of pasta side-by-side on wax paper to prevent them from sticking. Place a layer of tomato sauce in a large baking pan. Cover completely with a layer of pasta, then ricotta and mozzarella slices.

Top with sauce and cross another layer of pasta. Add half of the beef and cover with sauce. Add another layer of pasta and top with potato slices and peas. Top with sauce again. Add the rest of the beef and top with remaining sauce. Bake at 300°F for 30 minutes. Slays 8. *Optional:* add ½ teaspoon of T-Roy's Ass Bitin' Hot Sauce.

NEWS PAIRING: A California man Saran wrapped $17,000 in cash to a girdle he was found wearing after murdering his in-laws on Christmas Eve.

CHAPTER 6

BAGELS AND LOCKS

When it comes to food, convicts are ingenious.
—Daniel Genis

The federal prison system had a meltdown in 1995. It began in Talladega, Alabama where hundreds of armed inmates took over the jail. The government struck back by locking down every federal penitentiary, forcing even us Otisvillians to remain in our cubes.

My new home, Unit #5, was in a building where living cubes, versus cells, were the standard. There wasn't extra space, but the quarters were open air. The hundred here had the freedom to move around, but we all shared one window that framed the outside forest. Benny, known as "The Mayor of Hoboken," resided here since 1977, making him the original Otisvillain.

I was planted in a room with two salty nuts for three days; fortunately we were not packed in like sardines. Benny was a bald, brash Albanian who I stayed in touch with after my release. Lin, a Chinese teen who was wheelchair-bound from a street shooting, fashioned chess pieces out of candy wrappers. I admired that talent, and helped Lin out when I could.

Lockdown had us pooling together items from our lockers (or pantries, as Benny called them). The single microwave warmed our midnight munchies. Canned fish, noodles, and eggs stolen from the kitchen provided nutrition. Meals were brought in on rolling carts, kinda like room service.

Benny would throw down one of his T-shirts as a tablecloth. Kitchen Cop ("KC") Louie served with German Shepherd, Fury, and the other bitch, Greta, in tow. (If I had to choose who to be locked down with, I'd pick the dog.) Louie clearly took joy in steamrolling the cart over the hill of Fritos and Doritos Benny and I rationed on the floor.

The KCs now had to cook for a thousand men with no help. Kitchen Cops were all chefs, but Louie was a bad one whose food mirrored his sour personality. Lockdown breakfast was metallicy hard-boiled eggs, a bagel whose flavor was chemicalized by its cellophane wrapper, and a tot-sized box of Cheerios. The sack lunch sucked, too: one cold cheese sandwich, two slices of fried bologna, and a mystery meat that only the toughest lifer could stomach.

This sorry scene played out again at dinner. Hope seemed lost until Muslim guard, Teresa, rounded the corner with Carvel Flying Saucer Ice Cream sandwiches. (Honestly at first I thought it was a mirage.) They were served to keep the cons cool, and it worked for a New York minute. By day three, we began thinking outside the cube and concocted our own lockdown lunches.

Once Benny fashioned up a 'stinger,' we'd have hot water. He'd simply strip plastic from an extension cord, separate the wires, and cut a wee bit of wood from Lin's wheelchair. Benny would then insert the stinger into a paint bucket filled with water and BOOM: hot pasta for two.

There was no deep fry thermometer, just a felon's weathered finger to test if the oil was scalding. The sauce was cobbled from peppers, canned mackerel, and breakfast sausages. A con in the next cube made fried chicken by stinging hot oil inside an old trash can. The competition in here was fierce.

I wondered how many lockdowns I would face in the next ten years. Once my six-month restriction was lifted, Mom could visit. For this stubborn Italian woman, feeding me on the inside was as paramount to her sanity as eating her delicious dishes was to mine.

RECIPE: COLD STUFFED CUBES

8 oz. package of cream cheese
4 slices of bread of your choice
2 chunks of unsliced cheese of your choice
½ lb. of sliced cold cuts of your choice
1 tsp. capers
1 tsp. crushed garlic
toothpicks

Cut the four pieces of toasted/untoasted bread into sixteen quarters. Whip the cream cheese, crushed garlic and capers into a smooth spread. Butter the squares of bread with the mixture. Cube the cheese into quarters. Wrap a piece of deli meat around the squares of cheese and place between the small bread slices. Secure with toothpicks. Locks down a meal for 4.

NEWS PAIRING: The $1,000 bagel from the Westin Hotel Times Square includes white truffle cream cheese, goji berry-infused Riesling wine jelly, and edible gold leaf flakes.

CHAPTER 7

FISHIN' COUSINS

Sell a man a fish, he eats for a day. Teach a man how to fish,
you ruin a wonderful business opportunity.
—Karl Marx

Stavros and Nicky, aka The Greek Brothers, began their lives of crime looting swordfish out of the Mediterranean. The boys tried catching bluefin tuna, but the seven-hundred-pound, seven-foot creatures were too smart and fast for them. A third of the seafood in this country is harvested illegally, so of course the twosome was in on the grab.

With plenty of fish in the sea, they traded up to stealing striped bass off the coast of Manhattan and selling it at Mafia-run Fulton's Market downtown. One summer day, the Coast Guard found hot bass on board, not stuffed with onions, peppers, or breadcrumbs, but cocaine. Major blow.

The Greek Brothers reminded me so much of my cousins Frankie and Freddie, also enemies of the ocean. Those connivers once won a family fishing competition by jamming a sinker weight down a bass' throat, making it heavier and winning the game. Those two stank.

Unlike Nicky and Stavros, they hated each other from inside the womb. Frankie was a true bastard, but he was a handsome dog. His "father," Uncle Bucky, was one ugly cat. We called him that because his buck teeth stuck out like two pieces of yellow Chiclets gum. He also had this weird, narrow jaw that Freddie inherited.

The guys would come by once a month with Aunt Connie. They'd storm the kitchen and double down on Mom's chicken cacciatore. Then they'd scam the best seats in our living room for TV. There were nights I'd lay awake plotting young revenge. Fate interceded one afternoon when my chemistry kit blew Freddie's eyebrows straight off. He splattered blueberry pie all over Mom's white dress, charging through our house in horror.

Freddie found himself in loan shark waters years later, and was ultimately deboned. Money hungry Frankie, the fruit of adultery? I'll get to him later.

RECIPE: MEDITERREAN SEA BASS-TARD

2 sea bass, scaled and gutted
1 jar roasted red peppers, drained and sliced
1 red onion
4 garlic cloves
½ cup Kalamata olives
¼ cup toasted pine nuts
2 tbsp. olive oil
1 lemon

Heat the oven to 350°F. In a pan, sauté the garlic, onions, and peppers in one tablespoon of olive oil. Slice up half a lemon, add and set the mix aside. In a large buttered baking dish, place the sea bass skin side down, brush with remaining olive oil, and bake for five minutes. Bait with pine nuts and olives and cook for another five minutes. Add the pepper mixture. Hook the cooked fish up with parsley and the remaining speared lemon. Floats food for 4. *Optional:* Add a Dozen Cousins' Bone Broth Simmered Rice.

NEWS PAIRING: 'Surströmming' is banned on most airlines because the fermented, canned Swedish fish is potentially explosive.

CHAPTER 8

SLING BLADE

Tinned food is a deadlier weapon than the machine gun.
—George Orwell

"Jack Macking" places canned foods inside socks to concoct fast, heavy-hitting prison weapons. (Cucumbers work, too.) Water Bombing is another fluid, felonous idea: fill a garbage bag with five gallons of water and let it fly from the top of a prison unit at 80 mph. Sculpting cut-throat, spiky 'shivs' out of hard candy also deserves dishonorable mention. Nothing sparks creativity like a man locked in a cell.

I was having an odd lump on my back examined in the infirmary when the newest victim of the Tuna Can Caper was admitted for a pound of stitches. He had attempted to use the metal lid of a tuna fish can to slit his throat. With its barbed, jagged edges and flexibility to be slung like a blade, this saber often became the third wheel in many a coop quarrel. This deadly, con-made weapon is not one of my cubemates' pot pipes sculpted out of a horseradish tube.

Blood noodled down the victim's front, coiling his aging chest hair. I almost tossed my Wheaties, and I'm a convicted felon. I've employed cayenne pepper to stop kitchen cuts from bleeding, but I hoped the hospital would take a more medical approach.

The Creek Brothers ___e both there, and in chorus rang out how ___nd stuffing sea life was fine, but not this ___sn't the least bit fazed. She cleaned up the ___true, come-hither caregiver. ___an or you'll find yourself sleeping with

Purchase (yours to keep ☺)

Jou

RECIPE: XTRA SHARP CHEDDAR MELTS

4 slices of extra sharp cheddar cheese
4 slices of sourdough bread
2 cans white albacore tuna in olive oil
½ cup ketchup
4 tbsp. mayonnaise
2 tbsp. sweet relish
2 tbsp. orange juice
2 tbsp. lemon juice
1 tbsp. butter
1 tsp. capers
1 tsp. dill weed
1 tsp. Tabasco sauce
Coarse black pepper

Drain the tuna thoroughly and place in a bowl. Stir in mayonnaise, relish, capers, and dill. Whip until creamy. Squeeze in the orange and lemon juice. Add pepper to taste. Stir. Refrigerate. In a buttered pan, grill four pieces of cheese open-faced on two slices of bread. When brown, remove and doctor up a cold scoop of the tuna fish salad atop the sandwich. Close with a second piece of toasted bread. Use a sharp knife to slice in half, and bleed ketchup all over the melt. Treats 2. *Optional:* pair with Screamin' Salt and Vinegar Goldfish Crackers.

NEWS PAIRING: A man was cooked to death inside a Bumble Bee Tuna plant after becoming trapped inside a pressure cooker with 12,000 pounds of fish.

CHAPTER 9

SWEET AS HELL

I was in love with a beautiful blonde once. She drove me to drink.
That's the one thing I'm indebted to her for.
—W. C. Fields

Head RN Nurse Blackie was a beautiful, buxom, backseat blonde. The only thing missing to crown her Miss Minnesota was hay in her hair. Despite her apple red lips, nobody could physically get close to her because her breath was hotter than she was. Blackie was known to dispense a kind of sugar-coated nursing to my black brothers behind bars. She took a lot of risks, lacked morality, drank like a sailor, and swore like a madman. She was also a pretty decent person.

Easy to talk to – and with an easier bedside manner – Blackie was just an awful nurse. The fair-haired Florence Nightingale once took my blood pressure and my arm was so bruised I couldn't lift a roast bird out of the oven at dinner. She often reeked of liquor, but the booze was a blessing because it masked her hellacious halitosis. There wasn't much she was good at except turning men on from a distance. Blackie always had a positive attitude and free-spiritedly went commando part-time. I know because she'd be minus a panty line, and we'd all be plus a hard-on.

Stew cleaned and mopped the floors of the Otisville hospital up the hill, next to the jail. They shined so much you could see your sick self in the reflection. He was serving twenty years for carjacking and kidnapping, despite his victim bashing him in the face with her Mercedes tire iron. She did manage to escape, and left a pink scar on his black forehead. He referred to it as "the wrath of the white woman."

But Stew was hot for snowy-haired caucasian chicks, so Blackie strutting around sick bay without undies was straight up poetic. The undocumented vitamin shots she poked Stew with twice a week gave him further rise; he'd win weightlifting contests and collect cases of Orange Crush after squatting 700 pounds.

Stewart's janitorial prowess was not appreciated by the staff after Polaroids of Blackie's heart-shaped derriere were uncovered deep inside his locker. Rumor was Jesus ratted him out, because stealing other people's joy was also one of his crimes. Since our off-color nurse didn't explain the bruise marks on her prisoner-of-love, they were deemed drug tracks, and Stew was shipped out, sans barbells and blondes.

The ravishing, randy RN was reprimanded by Warden Keyes. Inmates nicknamed him "Denzel" because of his confidence, good looks, and way with words. It's safe to say Blackie enjoyed getting the shaft from him.

The one thing Blackie had right about nursing was not getting emotionally attached to her patients. She swept Stew under the rug, proving bonds in the brig are easily broken.

RECIPE: NURSE BLACKIE'S HEART-SHAPED SUGAR BUNS

2 eggs
4½ cups flour
1 cup warm milk
⅓ cup melted butter
⅓ cup room temperature butter
½ cup white & brown sugar
2½ tbsp. cinnamon
2½ tsp. yeast
1 tsp. salt
1 jar Filthy's Black Cherries

Preheat the oven to 350°F. Place the milk and yeast in a large bowl and let sit for 5 minutes. Add white sugar, melted butter, salt, and eggs. Mix and add in flour. Cover with a towel and let sit for two hours in a warm area. Roll out the dough on a flour-dusted surface into six-inch long, one-inch wide pieces. Slice black cherries and place atop dough. Twist the pieces into heart shapes, and place on a baking sheet two inches apart. Spread the butter on them and pinch a twosome of cinnamon and brown sugar over the buns. Bake for 15 minutes or until golden brown. Tantalizes 12. *Optional:* pair with Cockburn's Dessert Wine.

NEWS PAIRING: A beautiful Ghanaian nurse was murdered by a jealous colleague who poisoned her hospital lunchroom food.

CHAPTER 10

THE INDIAN'S LIVER

During prohibition, I was forced to live on nothing but food and water.
—W. C. Fields

I was still living in Unit #5, which also housed fifteen dialysis patients. They were privy to an outside hospital every week for treatment. This included one unfortunate, American Indian alcoholic named Daniel. His job was to shine and polish all the prison floors. I called him "Chief Pontiac" because his hulking size reminded me of my first car, a lime green Pontiac Star Chief. Jesus called him Brownie because Jesus was a dick.

Daniel was a loner who guzzled floor wax to get high. Once in a while he'd ask me for potatoes, oranges, and apples from the kitchen. Though a con, I was no pro yet on inmate moves. So thinking it was a bid to eat healthier, I always handed over the goods. Daniel had grown squash, corn, and beans back home; the healthy trinity was celebrated in his culture as "The Three Sisters." O Brother, Where Art Thou now? Up the river, making moonshine.

Where there's a will, there's a way to get smashed. When cooler life gives you lemons, add fruit, sugar, and bread and make Pruno, the convict's cocktail of choice. Often toxic with notes of botulism, prison wine is usually concocted with fruit cocktail, cake frosting, candy, ketchup, and milk. Its taste has been described as "an orange dipped in tap water from Chernobyl."

When a smell worse than Blackie's breath erupted, it meant the Chief had burped the plastic Pruno bag from inside the shitter, where he kept it warm and fermenting. He'd smash lumps out of the liquid like he was kneading dough, using his T-shirt as a strainer. Daniel would trade shots of his secret stash for cigs, ramen, or Little Debbie Chocolate Moon Pies. I saw a murderer hold his nose while he gulped it. My cubemate Joey manned up and wolfed it down. I was out; being tanked on toilet vino meant a month in the SHU.

Jarvis Masters is an African American Buddhist on San Quentin's Death Row. He penned the award-winning poem *Recipe for Prison Pruno,* fusing ingredients for jailhouse wine with his own death sentence announcement. The poetry is indicative of Pruno as an ingrained part of lockup life:

Take ten peeled oranges,
Jarvis Masters, it is the judgment and sentence of this court,
One 8 oz. bowl of fruit cocktail,
that the charged information was true,
Squeeze the fruit into a small plastic bag,
and the jury having previously, on said date,
And put the juice along with the mash inside,
found that the penalty shall be death,
Add 16 oz. of water and seal the bag tightly.

Maybe clink cooks are ahead of their time. Mainstream markets now offer a wide selection of pricey, trendy fermented foods, like toasted mesquite vinegar, ginger beets, wakame seaweed sauerkraut, soybean paste, and pickled potato fries. But beware: fermented veggies can be rotten. Six workers in India drowned after falling into a giant vat of ketchup, overcome by the fumes from the fermenting vegetables.

Evidence of alcoholic beverages made from fruit, honey, and rice date back to China, 7000 BCE. The following recipe teaches the ancient art of fruit fermentation (we left the wine-making to the experts).

RECIPE: PHIL'S PALATABLE PRUNO

Fermented Orange Juice:
    6 peeled oranges
    1 cup filtered water
    ½ tsp. sea salt
    ⅛ cup of whey

Add:
    1 cup dry white wine
    ⅛ cup soda water
    1 lemon zest
    1 tsp. lemon zest
    Organic cinnamon

Juice the half-dozen oranges, with pulp. Fill a quart-sized Mason jar half way with the fresh orange juice. Add 1 cup of purified water, leaving two inches of space. Add the sea salt and whey. Secure the lid and let sit for 24 hours.

After a day of fermenting, whip the juice, wine, lemon zest, soda water, and ice in a blender for two minutes. Pour into a wine glass and top with organic cinnamon. Bags drinks for 3.

NEWS PAIRING: Eight Arizona inmates ran up a $500,000 hospital bill after their cell-made Pruno gave them botulism poisoning.

CHAPTER 11

LET'S PLAY HIDE THE CUCUMBER

Vegetarian ... an old Indian word meaning "lousy hunter."
—Andy Rooney

Bobby's bushy, gray eyebrows framed his pale face. He was blonde before Mother Nature and Father Time gave him a makeover at Otisville. Now his skin was gritty, his hair salt and pepper.

Warden Keyes turned an empathetic eye to Bobby who, like himself, was a wounded NYPD officer. Keyes was maimed during the much publicized Bronx shootout of '86, where half a dozen cops were murdered. Former officers were almost always housed in protective custody units, but Bobby's time with the department wasn't exactly true blue, so the warden placed him in general pop.

Bobby had lost his right leg in an off-duty car accident. The department hadn't provided him decent medical insurance, or offered him his job back. To get revenge, he fed the mob scraps about police taps and surveillance videos. Sentenced to ten years in the Camp, he'd become my talented assistant, since he once moonlighted as a chef at the Waldorf Astoria in the city.

I taught my bitter friend how to play pinochle, and he taught me how to really cook. Despite walking with crutches or on a prosthetic leg, he was cool. He sported John Lennon-like round glasses, and cut the sleeves from his shirts to magnify his meaty biceps.

Lunch at Otisville was usually sliced Donkey Dick (cold cuts). I mainly consumed ramen noodles topped with my favorite custom concoctions: peanut butter & olive oil or hot sauce & mustard. I soon landed a job on the serving line forking out desserts, and managed to avoid trouble, i.e., giving two slices of pie to one con. The Godfather got me the gig.

Ruffian Marat Balagula ran the largest black market food co-op in the Ukraine. This set him up to immigrate to the States and become the Godfather of the Russian American Mafia. He was always good to me, even helping to settle my poker debts. Why? I'd hand over sweets off my personal tray—bread pudding, custard, jelly donuts—and funnel Reese's Peanut Butter Cups I charged to my commissary account. Marat was one of the sweetest gangsters I ever knew.

Bobby and I started to stuff and steal like mad from the kitchen. I laughed every single time he hid veggies in his hollow leg. He could get eight-to-ten cucumbers down inside that thigh. He'd feign pain, retrieve his crutches, and carry out his loaded-up leg like a Zabar's grocery bag. Our healthy haul also included zucchini, bell peppers, and carrots. One onion could be trafficked for three postage stamps.

Tomatoes were always scarce. Years later at the Camp, I suggested that inmates start growing their own every summer, and we did. Gardening made us all feel calm and meditative. We started with four little plants, and the garden remained fertile for ten years, until I was uprooted to the Florida halfway house. To give credit where it's due, Jesus turned out to be a fruitful farmer who cared for the plants like he did his white rat, Maria.

Hauling edibles back to our cubes one day, Teresa surprised us with a body search. Ahh, a search for tomatoes, by a tomato. Teresa recovered enough veggies to build a salad bar: greens in my socks, pants, boxers, and jacket. Bobby scrambled on the floor, retrieving the fallen produce, while The Greek Brothers imitated him, hobbling around like three-legged contestants in a potato sack race. In a poised, conclusive voice that reminded me of my daughter, Teresa leveled the twins with threats of permanent separation. They retreated like pouting teenagers.

The Greek Brothers looked nothing alike but had matching, maddening falsetto voices. Both forty, Nicky looked twenty-five, with a chiseled jaw and full head of hair. Stavros' mane was majorly thinning, and topped a stocky, heavy body (think Colin Farrell and Fred Flintstone).

Teresa called in cocky, Kitchen Cop Louie to handle me. He was a small man; his twisted escargot-ears looked like two snails crawled up into his empty head and retired. The only ample thing about him was his attitude. Louie shoved me back into the kitchen where I was forced to unload my stash in front of the other inmates. That was almost as painful as his pitiful jokes, "How do you know a prison guard is gay? By the smell of his mustache." Even bad humor can be nourishing in the clink.

Sometimes the slammer can surprise you. Out of nowhere, the (Italian) Kitchen Cop I worked under fished me out of the serving line and promoted me. I was now part of the kosher kitchen, where conditions and food were much improved. My work experience was just making pasta at home in Brooklyn, but it was all about who you knew, and I knew Marat.

In most lockup movies, the star survives by honing a skill to stay sharp. The painter in *Escape from Alcatraz;* the librarian in *The Shawshank Redemption;* Paul Newman's charm in *Cool Hand Luke.* Now, Phil Longo, the cook at Otisville, with a little crumb of clout.

RECIPE: BOBBY'S BITTER LEG OF LAMB

1 shankless leg of lamb
6 quartered cloves of garlic
4 sprigs of fresh rosemary
3 tbsp. olive oil
fresh ground pepper
kosher salt
bitter dill dipping sauce

Preheat the oven to 325°F. Poke holes in the lamb and hide the garlic pieces by concealing them in the meat. Rub the roast with olive oil, rosemary, salt, and pepper. Cook 20 minutes per pound for medium rare. Compliment with plum pepper jelly. For bitter dipping sauce, mix lemon and lime juice with sour cream and dill. A dinner stash for 6.

NEWS PAIRING: An argument over groceries was to blame for a North Carolina altercation where a woman left her wheelchair to beat a man with her prosthetic leg.

CHAPTER 12

STEWING IN IT

Know what's a strange feeling? Sitting on the toilet eating a chocolate bar.
—George Carlin

Lincoln had milk chocolate-colored skin and a head shaped like a little eggplant. Entrepreneurial and British, he always had his finger in the pie, picking up contraband groceries, running food errands for guards 'n gangsters, and getting the Jews kosher grub from nearby New Square. Seemed appropo his nickname was Linc.

Lincoln taught me about the lucrative and illegal Smokie trade in the UK, which landed him at Otisville. Carcasses of sheep, lambs, goats, and pigs would be blowtorched after slaughter, and the charred, under-cooked meat sold as exotic fare. The delicacy can pass on disease, but its rich smoky taste delighted Brits and Africans. Linc sold this delicacy in England for years, until he learned about the hearty demand for it in Brooklyn.

I was leery to befriend Lincoln, as white and black in the pen were impossibly opposing. I wasn't racist. I just never talked to a black person until I was sixteen. In my community, being white and Italian was the word and the way. But I didn't see color when I looked at Linc. Just a cool-cat who would become this man's best friend.

One visitor's day, Lincoln's family was a no-show. Although chicken was hard to come by, I always froze a few emergency breasts, which I now shared with him. Lincoln once said I could prepare him anything except a wedding cake and he'd love it. (Linc's friend on the outside was supposed to look after his spouse and son, but straight up stole his wife.) Regardless of how different we all were, we were really just hungry, angry, lonely men.

Lincoln earned his high school GED inside prison walls and never stopped taking classes or borrowing books. He enrolled in courses ranging from sewer sanitation to criminal law, and even inspired me to take an advanced cooking class. Both a businessman and people pleaser, he was happy to go the extra mile for any hungry yard bird on a budget.

Linc was addicted to action. Why not? Almost every inmate comes with some monkey on his back. If buying or selling drugs in jail was your bag, you could flush any chance of keeping your original sentence. Guests also had to be pretty gutsy to smuggle in narcotics. Bloodthirsty police dogs aside, friends would have to excrete the condom-wrapped loot into a toilet after ramming the hidden package up their rear.

Once the "eagle had landed," Lincoln and Joey would retrieve the load over at the Otisville sewage plant half a mile away. Joey was a man who brushed his teeth with baking soda and despised the shitty job. Dirt was not his scene, but drugs were, so he continued with the crappy work.

RECIPE: DIRTY RICE WITH CHICK PEES

3 cups wild brown rice
1 cup shiitake mushrooms
1 cup chickpeas
½ cup chopped red bell pepper
½ cup chopped red onion
¼ cup poppy seeds
3 tbsp. soy sauce
2 tbsp. olive oil
1 tbsp. sesame oil

Retrieve peppers, mushrooms, onions, chickpeas and olive oil and sauté in a pan. Cook the wild rice and set aside. Flush out the soy sauce and sesame oil and stir into the rice. Mix in veggies and sprinkle with black and white poppy seeds to taste. Works for 4. *Optional*: bust out Toxic Waste Hot Sauce for flavor.

NEWS PAIRING: An ice cream shop in Tokyo has become famous for its Poop Ice Cream, a load of soft-swirled chocolate served in a toilet-themed container.

CHAPTER 13

WOULD JESUS STEAL THAT ORANGE?

I worked hard in the (jailhouse) kitchen ... I couldn't cook before.
—Singer James Brown

Jesus was a cat burglar and jewel thief, but no pussy. Eighteen and boney, he'd been climbing into Bronx windows since he was big enough to break one open. He idolized his mother, who warbled into the wee hours at Manhattan nightclubs to provide for her boys. Jesus rarely took off her ruby pinky ring that he was somehow able to keep in lockup.

The glamorous Mexican songstress always took him with her to work. She feared he'd be teased—or worse—by his kin because of the big red birthmark jammed above his eyes. Jesus's mother would pacify the boy with bricks of Valrhona Mexican chocolate, and he'd sit backstage and eat his feelings. His mother died when he was a kid, leaving him to be raised by his browbeating brothers. No doubt his first piece of jewelry was a house key latched around his neck.

Jesus started off stealing family trinkets, but his taste matured. He landed at Otisville after attempting to rob the Smithsonian's National Gem Collection. Friendless and forlorn, nobody messed with The Mole. He may have been a teenager, but he was rumored to be the cousin of drug king, El Chapo. If you wanted hard-to-get contraband, you went soft and looted your lady's lingerie on their next visit as his payment.

I had to work with Jesus in the kosher kitchen, where tuna, cottage cheese, and cold beans were the chosen foods. My work team topped off with the arrival of Eddie Antar, known to East Coast TV coach potatoes as "Crazy Eddie." Famous for his fast-talking TV commercials, Dan Aykroyd played him in *Saturday Night Live* spoofs. I recall Eddie actually liking the dining hall cottage cheese, which was bland, boring, and bitter – but he was not.

Crazy Eddie got a ten-year sentence and was fined $60M for stock fraud. His wife would pick up my mother in Brooklyn, and they would drive together to see their brig boys. Eddie made the front page when his second wife gave birth while he was inside. Odd, as conjugal visits weren't allowed. But Eddie was crazy as a fox. He had frozen his sperm prior to prison.

Jesus quartered oranges as part of a scheme to screw the Jews out of their fruit. The least ripe baubles would go out on the trays, and the rest of the juice would be smuggled out in cottage cheese containers and sold for some quick bread. Another juicy way to get contraband out – food, electronics, whatever – involved kitchen inmates refreshing the salad bar (lettuce, carrots, maybe a radish) and placing the goods inside a serving pan for retrieval. I once saw a cell phone sink to the bottom of a pork stew.

Fresh OJ was killer contraband. Not as popular as mind-numbing Pruno, but you'd pocket ten bucks for twelve pulpy ounces. I might have complained, but just last week, Jesus locked a squealer's head in between two steel rods of a cooking stand. The dishy Greek Brothers had spilled the story, prompting KC Louie to show up to our next shift.

I tossed the fruit skins into trash cans like kosher basketballs, as the contraband king's sticky situation would bring me down, too. No score: Louie leered around and found the hulls. He grabbed onto my apron and, having stuck one of the orange rinds inside his lips, acted out Brando's death scene from *The Godfather*. I couldn't believe what I was seeing, but I was sure of what I heard: Demotion. I was stuck on the main service line for another year.

Being a cartel cousin made lockup life more manageable, as Jesus kept his job and I lost mine. Bobby replaced me in the kosher kitchen, no longer having to stew and sauce for Nicky and Stavros, who he doubly hated. Moral of the story? Thou shalt not steal, peel, or squeal in the can.

RECIPE: JEWELED MUFFINS

¼ cup blueberries
¼ cup cranberries
¼ cup minced carrots
¼ cup minced green jalapeños
¼ cup melted butter
2 cups all-purpose flour
2 eggs
1 cup milk
½ cup sugar
½ bag chocolate chips
1 tbsp. baking powder
1 tsp. Mexican vanilla
½ tsp. kosher salt

Preheat the oven to 400°F. Blend the dry ingredients together, including the kosher salt. Toss and stir in chocolate chips, blueberries, cranberries, minced carrots, and minced green jalapeños, as the flavors work well together. Mix the liquids and add to the now-colorful dry ingredients. Whisk together like crazy for 20 seconds. Grease the muffin pan and fill each section up two thirds. Place in the oven for 15–20 minutes. Steals the heart of 4. *Optional:* mash in orange jewel yams for moister muffins.

NEWS PAIRING: Oranges in *The Godfather* represent harbingers of death: The Don buys oranges before being ambushed, and they spill onto the sidewalk as he's shot, and Sonny drives past a billboard promoting oranges before he is killed.

CHAPTER 14

YOU HAVE TO EAT A PECK OF DIRT BEFORE YOU DYE

Many of my friends are good chefs. Kind of like being in the Mafia.
—Anthony Bourdain

The song "You're So Vain" was written about my former roommate, Joey. Well, it could have been. I would watch in amazement as he took hard time grooming in front of reflective, makeshift mirrors. He was a handsome con with a perfect chevron mustache. This was the only thing he had in common with Gandhi.

Joey had his mother, Gianna, sneak in black hair dye to cover up his grays. He perfected his lockup manicure using Hellmann's mayo for lotion, and a matchbook's striking surface as the nail file. He taught me how to use olive oil to slick my hair back Gordon Gekko-style. Looking sharp was vital to this dangerous, magnetic stud.

Joey was born in America, but his family was still part of the 'Ndrangheta Mafia (Italian police recently caught two 'Ndrangheta bosses who hung cooking pots on their bunker wall alongside firearms). Joey was moved back to Calabria when he was six. Seventeen years later, he was inducted into The Family, and a few after that, he moved into an Italian jail with access to a wine cellar.

Joey's final crime was smuggling the world's most expensive spice, saffron, out of the Middle East. He'd arrange for its transport from Iran to Italy; there the gold powder would be placed into cans labeled as tomatoes and shipped to America. He got caught yellow-handed and did a five-year sentence in Naples, only to be deported to the Land of the Free and serve another five years for the same crime.

Gianna regularly snuck in Panettone, Nutella, hard salami, and Parmigiano-Reggiano when her bodacious bambino was moved to the Camp. Joey was an excellent cook – the crème de la crème – until Bobby arrived. His puttanesca sauce was the best I have ever tasted. His trick was peppering in golden raisins and butter nuts, stolen from the local squirrels. I think Joey favored this sauce for its history as a quick bite for ladies of the night.

RECIPE: JOEY'S RAISIN' PUTTANESCA (AS SERVED BY PHIL)

12 unpitted black olives
6 cloves of chopped garlic
1 lb. spaghetti
1 diced onion
1 red bell pepper
1 cup ricotta
1 can diced tomatoes
1 small can of anchovies
¼ cup olive oil
¼ cup golden raisins
¼ cup capers
2 tbsp. pine nuts

In a large skillet, sauté garlic in olive oil. Add onion, bell pepper, anchovies, and olives. Leave on low heat until the onion is caramelized. Sneak in the pine nuts, capers, and tomatoes; cover, simmer and let the mix do the time (fifteen minutes). Remove from heat and stir in the ricotta and raisins. Dish out over spaghetti and garnish with parmesan. Satisfies 4.

NEWS PAIRING: Artist Lauren Garfinkel's *Putinesca* is an edible canvas of Vladimir Putin, created with spaghetti and puttanesca sauce.

"THANKS — THAT LOOKS DELICIOUS —
CHARGE IT TO MY ROOM WOULD YOU?

PART 3
IN THE OVEN

CHAPTER 15

SOLICITATION AND THE FINE ART OF VISITOR'S DAY

*Food has taken the place of sex in my life. I've just
had a mirror put over my kitchen table.*
—Rodney Dangerfield

Visitor's Day (VD) inside was a special occasion. Louie would show up to "inspect the fresh meat" cloaked in a hospital mask, which he said was for germs. Check.

Joey looked forward to VD but I didn't, as our cell would be reeking of Drakkar Noir for a week. He soaked himself in the weird leather/licorice/lavender cologne when his young Asian girlfriend visited. He'd rise and shine at 5 a.m., steal an iron out of the maintenance closet and perfectly crease his prison pants.

The visitor area was a sea of stackable plastic yellow chairs, little rays of sunshine in the windowless room. Greta perched herself on the raised platform to supervise like a bird of prey, overseeing twenty-five inmates and their company. VD guests weren't strip-searched if they didn't seem suspicious, like my mom and her girdled pasta. Greta authorized one snuggle-less hug when your peeps arrived, and one when they left.

Visiting hours wound down by 3 p.m. Greta's orange lips were jabbering Teresa's head off, who was also on call. Nothing about Teresa seemed familiar today. For one, she was smiling. But her hair looked sticky and crimpy, like a Jersey girl from the boardwalk. Her makeup looked like it was applied with a roller brush, not a common Middle Eastern look. I had unknowingly just met her brazen alter ego, "Risa." This tougher personality surfaced at the oddest times, and we would meet many times over the next ten years.

Sex in federal pens was almost always a solo act. Sculpting an artificial vagina out of a rubber glove (a Fifi), masturbating (Code 21), or gay sex (making tortillas) was the closest you'd come. So when a couple next to me was preparing to lay the track (cram in a quickie) it was a wild feast for the senses.

A skinny dude with long braids was planted in a chair with a huge woman bent over him. She lifted up her XL coat, sat on his XS junk, and started humping and thumping. Joey and I used our Godless intuition and stood up to shield them from Greta. The fun lasted less than a minute, but the thin man remained our big phat hero for months.

Otisville cops took contact seriously. Once my daughter was leaving, and I kissed my hand and placed it on her cheek. Jesus squealed to Greta and I was sent to the SHU for a week. I'd have gone on a hunger strike, but the Hole already guaranteed an empty stomach: PB&J for lunch and one slice of bologna for dinner. Not even half a coconut like Steve McQueen scored in solitary in *Papillion*.

RECIPE: BIG PHAT QUICKIE CREAMPUFFS

4 eggs
1 cup flour
1 cup water
1 cup heavy whipping cream
½ cup butter
1 tbsp. sugar
1 ounce Wild Turkey bourbon

Preheat the oven to 375°F. In a large saucepan, boil water and butter. Add flour and stir until the dough forms a ball. Add eggs and beat until smooth. Place large, rectangular-sized pieces on a cookie sheet four inches apart. Bake for 40 minutes, or until golden brown. Insert a skinny toothpick into the center of the puffs. Pull it out without streaks of batter and you're good to go.

For the filling, whip the cream in a mixing bowl and gradually add sugar until stiff peaks are formed. Fold in the bourbon and refrigerate for no less than two hours. Place the filling in a piping bag and, with a finger, make a hole on the top of the cream puffs. Squeeze the white filling in, serve and enjoy. Makes 6 plump desserts.

NEWS PAIRING: A pregnant woman was arrested in San Quentin's visitor's room when her baby bump turned out to be smuggled in peach cobbler.

CHAPTER 16

WHICH SIDE IS YOUR BREAD BUTTERED ON?

People don't take to skinny Mafia men.
—James Gandolfini

The next eight years, I was a resident of the "Otis Villas" down the hill. I was ready to move to the Camp, with my lean belongings and vain expectations: better food, privacy in the john, freedom to work out and walk outside anytime, cleaner rooms, and upgraded occupants.

Teresa escorted me on the cold, muddy jaunt. I was sure her earthiness and pretty consistent kindness would make the transition easier. But her demeanor that day was more hard-talking jailbird than a jailer. Alas, my chaperone was chatty, batty 'Risa', who I encountered a year back in the visitor's room. Teresa never wore her sexuality on her sleeve like Risa. Fish nor fowl, in the future I'd defend them both when harassed.

I didn't know what to expect from the Camp, but passing through real grass on the way there was a good start. Some guys from the prison were here now, all having been cool cons who didn't give the guards too much crap. Lin seemed happy to see me, despite my disfiguring his wheelchair for wood during lockdown.

My first stop at Camp was the washroom to wet my face. There I found my former prison pal Joey, splashing an acidic-smelling, discolored water on his face. I'd seen a stream of shit in the prison, but washing in pee pools? I avoided shaking hands when he surfaced, but the marvelous Mafioso was hard to say no to, especially since he was my new roommate.

I watched him admire himself in the reflective bottom of a 'borrowed' kitchen pot that night, and learned it was saffron water he bathed his face in earlier. I guess it tanned him. Was he trying to disguise himself? He was being targeted by Willie Potato here in the (nonviolent) Camp.

Potato was nicknamed after Chicago's Willie "Potatoes" Daddano, famous for torturing his victims with an ice pick. Sickly overweight and wheelchair-bound, Potato was adamant about Joey's demise. But it had to be cleared by the American mob bosses, as my pal Joey was a Mademan, meaning he had murdered for the mafia and was 100% Italian. These facts made him untouchable.

After failing to recruit the dangerous and inept Greek Brothers for the job, Willie met wheel-to-wheel with Lin, who was no killer, but would work for peanuts. But Lin wasn't cut out for hardcore crime; he squealed to the warden, who leaked it to the FBI, who reduced Lin's sentence for cooperating. What happened to Willie Potato I cannot say; my tongue would be tied.

Food, mafiosos, and murder are all tied up together. The Palace Chophouse in Newark was the execution site of Prohibition-era gangster, Dutch Schultz; Paul Castellano, head of the Gambino crime family, was killed in front of the entrance to Sparks Steak House in Midtown Manhattan. "Crazy Joe" Gallo of the Columbo family was murdered at Umberto's restaurant in New York, and Carmine Galante, boss of the Bonanno family, ate it at Joe & Mary's in Brooklyn.

RECIPE: CHINESE CHICKEN WHEELS WITH LEAKS

4 flour tortillas
2 chicken breasts
2 red peppers
¼ cup olive oil
1 tbsp. sesame oil
1 bunch of scallions
1 bunch of leeks

Thoroughly wash the chicken breasts and slice as thinly as possible. Sauté in a bath of Italian olive oil. Set aside. Finely chop the scallions, leeks, and red peppers and mix with the sesame oil. Place the chicken on a tortilla and smother with scallion and pepper mixture. Roll the tortilla into plastic wrap. Keep them cool for two hours. Unwrap and cut into two inch wheels. Targets a meal for 2. *Optional:* add sweet golden saffron threads to the olive oil to enrich the taste of the wheels.

NEWS PAIRING: A wheelchair-bound paraplegic made headlines for wrestling a thief to the floor and thwarting a robbery at a Vancouver Food Stop.

CHAPTER 17

AN URNING FOR COFFEE

I begin each day with coffee and obituaries.
—Bill Cosby

Noreen "Sip" O'Mally was a forty-five-year-old Irish woman who didn't look a day over sixty. Born in New York's Irish section, Pearl River, Sip was a drinker who was built like a moose: wide, thick, and tall. She had the demeanor of a wise elder, and swaggered with masculine energy.

O'Mally wore her red hair in an out-of-date beehive that often enhanced her bloodshot eyes and peachy skin. I'd monitor her mood based on the condition of that hive. The only thing more implausible was a Mafia mademan offering to coiffe it. She smiled when she sautéed sober, and her beefy fingers held up an enormous emerald ring. If it was real, it meant she also had big balls for wearing it to work.

I enjoyed Sip's company in the kitchen. She had a razor sharp wit and was a fanatic foodie. Everyone dug her cooking. Her recipes were creative, and unlocked tasty, contrasting flavors. You'd often find her at the Camp's java station, sipping her way back to sobriety.

Coffee was a nicety for campers and available round-the-clock. I bought the same red and white thermal mug from the commissary that all the cool cats had. I made "Lockup Latte" with a half-pint of milk and a really hot faucet. Just stick the small carton of milk under the hot water until steam rises. Pop it open, add instant coffee and a packet of pancake syrup, and be beamed to Starbucks. Sounds innocent enough, concocting coffees, yet I witnessed a con pitch a deadly fireball to a guard after lighting powdered creamer on fire.

One of Otisville's notable gangsters kept expensive Kopi luwak coffee hidden in his cube. He made me a cup once after running his Christmas Eve errands. Brew forever reminded me of home. Food can have heartbreaking associations.

I enjoyed taking my plaid mug outside to slurp on the tennis court. The sun would be on my face, with no one on my back. My 6 a.m. solitude one morning was interrupted by Teresa, frantically swatting and hissing a bee off her tea. Spilling my coffee, I captured the buzzard in one hand and, against her wishes, released it alive into the forest. Her toothy smile reminded me of my daughter's.

We dished on details that guards and inmates don't share. She reflected on her old life in Iran, and spoke of a twin sister, "the beautiful one," who was the apple of her dad's eye. Teresa's mood vacillated; she replayed sad scenes of being a bullied schoolgirl, and then happy ones about longing for American pizza. She confessed having tasted a halal version once, but her father forbade the meal, since pizza is never mentioned in the Koran.

Chewing the dysfunctional family fat got me thinking about Sheila. My extreme ex was an isolator who demanded all my attention. Outside of the occasional night she cooked, our marriage was plagued. Browning and broiling were the only times we ever came together.

RECIPE: TERESA'S HOT AND COLD HUMMUS

15 oz. can of chickpeas
3 cloves of minced garlic
2 tbsp. of tahini
2 tbsp. of sesame oil
1 tsp. of red pepper flakes
1 tsp. of cayenne pepper
4 pockets of pita bread
½ tsp. of coriander
½ cup of honey
Juice of 1 lemon

Drain and rinse the chickpeas. Combine all the ingredients, except the honey and pita, in a mixer and blend at high speed until smooth. Refrigerate overnight in a covered bowl. When ready, take pita slices out of the oven after warming and sharply cut into sister slices, or quarters. Top with the hummus spread, which can be served hot or cold, depending on your mood. A robust starter for 4. *Optional:* add a teaspoon of strong coffee to the hummus for a nutty smell.

NEWS PAIRING: A Minnesota man who ejaculated into his coworker's coffee was exonerated, as the accuser drank the morning brew despite noticing the odd, sour taste.

CHAPTER 18

FOOD STAMP

Tattoos transform us from raw animals to cooked, cultural beings.
—Claude Levi Strauss

Elon Alhadeff was a cunning Jewish doctor jailed for Medicare fraud. His square-rimmed glasses and perfect teeth didn't pin him as a clever criminal. We'd play cards and hustle inmates for sustenance and stamps. The Yarmulke-clad yardbird bore a tattoo, forbidden in his religion. He confessed he got Darth Vader inked on his arm to win the affection of his *Star Wars* loving young son.

Almost all men in the cooler come in with tats, or order a few up, courtesy of the penitentiary 'Ink Slinger.' I have a great white shark on my back, but had it done post-slammer. I didn't want a reminder of the keep etched on me for life.

The coop chef was a kindred friend to The Ink Slinger, who often ordered berries, corn syrup, and vinegar for his edible toolbox. I always handed them over, but I myself didn't want to dye. Once I offered a glass olive jar as an inkwell and it was well received. Tuna, ramen, or candy bars like Almond Joys or Kit Kats, were always popular goods cashed in for pen tats.

Color drained from foods doesn't last long as tat ink, but it works for those starving for short-term attention. Salt will preserve dark, natural stains like blueberry juice, like Civil War soldiers used for ink-art. Coffee grinds make a decent natural dye, unlike the sometimes-used noxious black soot left after melting a plastic prison meal tray.

Being inked up on the inside was always fashionable and boss: even Warden Keyes' left arm was sleeved in bright, army-themed art.

RECIPE: RATA-TATTOO-IE

4 cloves of garlic
1 cup diced eggplant
1 cup diced zucchini
1 cup yellow squash
1 cup diced beefsteak tomatoes
1 diced red bell pepper
1 package Portobello mushrooms
1 diced Bermuda onion
½ cup olive oil
Fresh sage, oregano, and basil
Salt and pepper

In a large saucepan, sauté the garlic in olive oil and add onions until caramelized. Toss in the diced red bell pepper, purple eggplant, green zucchini, and yellow squash. Cook until done. Add the tomatoes, mushrooms, herbs, salt, and pepper to taste. Draws in 4. *Optional:* add two tablespoons of Tinta de Sepia's culinary black squid ink to make the dish tastier and more picturesque.

NEWS PAIRING: Kellyanne Conway, counselor to former President Donald Trump, used "Blueberry" as her secret service code name.

CHAPTER 19

OREGA KNOW-IT-ALL

Only a fool argues with a skunk, a mule, or a cook.
—Cowboy saying

The closest KC Louie got to his French roots was flipping fries and picking up foreign floozies south of 14th Street. He'd rant about the beautiful broads he hooked up with from nearby Puss 'n Boots stripclub, but we knew inmate/Original Gangster Tommy Milo hired the girls in trade for private meals made by the hideous hash slinger.

Being French never stopped Louie's insulting rants about Teresa being Muslim, Lincoln's blackness, or me and Joey's Italian splendor. (No mystery why he left cartel-cousin Jesus alone.) He reminded me of my late Machiavellian brother Eddie; I never caught either of them in a truth.

As Louie clamored around in his NYPD baseball hat, it brought me back to Eddie, who once drew the city name "Pleiku" onto his own cap so he could parade as a Vietnam vet and find favor. I didn't wish my brother's death on anyone – a plane crash into a mountain – but if little Louie could just fly away … just fuck off and vanish.

Louie's overt disdain for me only grew when the Italian KC scored me yet another heady gig, now as Camp Cook. (Turns out I was in good company: Robert Downey, Jr., Kiefer Sutherland, and singer James Brown all held cookhouse jobs while serving time.)

Sip would often bug out of work with a Dublin-sized hangover, forcing Shrimpy down from the prison mountaintop to stand in at Camp. I prepared spaghetti and meat sauce for the men every other week, doubling down on oregano for extra flavor. But Louie insisted I stop using the spice; he saw it as exclusive to his pizza sauce recipe.

Cooking well for the guys started to matter to me. They loved spicy food, so I defied orders and overdid the oregano. In turn, Louie fried my ego in a double boiler: I'd now be lowered to assistant cook, earning twenty-five less clams a month. Bobby was now head cook. The only good news: only he could make institutionalized food taste almost gourmet, no piece of cake.

RECIPE: CRABBY LOUIE SALAD

1 lb. fresh Dungeness crab meat
8 cooked and chilled asparagus spears
8 artichoke hearts in olive oil, drained
3 boiled eggs cut in half
2 ripe tomatoes cut into wedges
Head of iceberg lettuce
Sprig of parsley
Pinch of oregano

Cover a plate with the lettuce leaves and build a pile of crab meat in the middle. Alternate the tomatoes, eggs, asparagus, and artichoke hearts around the mound. Use lemon wedges around the plate. Garnish lightly with chopped parsley and oregano. Present french dressing to guests, or do it Louie's way: mix mayo, chili sauce, onions, and peppers. Cooks up a meal for 2.

NEWS PAIRING: A Calgary mother was found guilty of criminal negligence when she refused to take her ill, seven-year-old son to the hospital, instead treating him with oregano oil.

CHAPTER 20

OSSO BITCHO

Cauliflower is nothing but cabbage with an education.
—Mark Twain

Part-time security cop and full-time shrew, Greta, doubled as Otisville's paralegal. She was obese as a pig, walked like a duck, and was blind as a bat. (She deserves clichés.) Her cantaloupe-colored lipstick and salt and pepper shaggy 'do were clearly an ode to Cruella De Vil. The strand of oversized pearls she wore every day were less Barbara Bush and more Lisa Simpson. These were her only she-habits.

Greta was a Stormtrooper and a tongue lasher who did more damage with her mouth in a morning than Howard Stern. My daughter said she smelled like a thrift store. A divorced, bitter eyesore, she was vicious to everyone but Joey, my smooth-talking cellmate who had the build and bulge of Tony Manero, and the air and hair of Michael Corleone.

After losing my first appeal for a reduced sentence, I phoned my lawyer, Ari. We knew the call would be taped, so he purposely declared himself an unfit attorney, giving me grounds for a second appeal. The judge ordered the recording to be preserved, so I felt confident when I went to Greta for my copy. The jar of rainbow jellybeans on her desk gave me hope she might have a sweet side.

Pissing in my cornflakes, she lied that the facility didn't record phone conversations. I harnessed my inner rage and politely asked about the sign above the inmate phone booth that read, "All conversations are being recorded." This was one of maybe three times in ten years I insisted on seeing the Warden.

When I stepped into Warden Keyes' office, I got the inmates' "Denzel" reference right away. The dude had copious suavé; his shiny, bald head complimented his coiffed goatee. He offered me a slice of the peach pie a local baked for him. My words said "Heavens, no" but my mouth said "Hell, yes."

I stayed focused and handed Keyes a copy of my attorney's phone bill, to prove our call took place. The warden agreed to have his office check it out. Peachy, until it came back that the tape had been "destroyed in error." The rest of my "hamburger," or ten-year sentence, would be served at Otisville.

Greta showed up at the Camp for dinner the following night. I denied the shrew service, so Louie ordered Bobby to plate her up ASAP. Holding a three-foot cooking ladle high-in-hand, he yielded the boss a brutish salute and began piling up her plate. Dragging me out of the kitchen, Louie warned Bobby that Fury would love to use his good leg as a bone.

Greta scarfed the steak Bobby over-peppered, courtesy of pink peppercorns from the trees (he could have opted for the poisoned mushrooms). When the spicing sent her out coughing, beef-loving Nurse Blackie devoured the rest. Some just like it hot.

Greta's grisly chipped tooth always brought me back to my younger brother, who slammed a door in my face and cracked my choppers when I was ten. My two front teeth had to be pulled and, as everyone knew, my family couldn't afford replacements. I was bullied at school for being broke and toothless. This created a gap in my confidence I would forever try to fill.

<u>RECIPE: FUGLY BISCUITS</u>

    2 cups all-purpose flour
    2 cups pecans or hazelnuts
    ¾ cup milk
    ½ cup shortening
    1 tsp. baking powder
    1 tsp. vanilla
    ½ tsp. salt
    ¼ tsp. cinnamon
    ¼ tsp. nutmeg

Toast and grind the nuts, but preserve their flavor. Add spices and set aside. Mix up sifted flour, salt, and baking powder in a large bowl. Add shortening in pieces and blend. Combine nut mixture and milk. Knead until workable. Drop uneven tablespoons onto the greased baking sheet. Cook at 300°F for thirty minutes or until golden brown. Don't let them get burnt. Sets up 16. *Optional:* brush with Miss Bee Haven's Honey for more appeal.

NEWS PAIRING: A Florida man with seven first degree murder convictions married his lawyer's paralegal on live TV. The newlyweds met every Saturday in the prison cafeteria.

CHAPTER 21

BIRDS OF A FEATHER GET MURDERED TOGETHER

My idea of fast food is a mallard.
—Ted Nugent

Otisville's pets were the feral cats shepherded by Jesus. The land around Camp was like The Wild Frontier. Once Grayson pried a bear cub out of a pine tree with our kitchen broom.

The grounds of Otisville were the summer home of migrating Canada geese. These large birds with their monster craps were a nuisance at best. After feeding tiny bread balls to fawns, Joey decided dinner would be goose, and he'd run the game himself.

The mademan acted like a madman, trying to throw blankets over their lanky heads. The birds looked like deadbeats trying to outrun the Mafia. Finally, Joey snapped a neck and brought the fowl into the kitchen. Together we plucked, feathered, and gutted the gander.

Angry about the goose abuse, and pissed he wasn't invited to eat any, Jesus told Greta that I had killed and cooked the bird. I was threatened with a month in the SHU if I didn't leave the fowl alone. (Goosing geese in New York is a federal offense.)

Fortunately, Joey confessed, setting the stage for my reprieve. I don't think I'd survive a month in solitary—the last guy came out with a trained cockroach he named Hank. I parted with the sesame cookies my sister Anita had baked as a 'thank you' to my rogue roomie.

The animal frenzy continued a week later on a sweltering day, when Lincoln and Joey eyed a thirty-pound snapping turtle with a patched green shell on the verdant grounds. Chief Pontiac said tortoise meat tasted like crab, so I was onboard when Linc coaxed it from the pond. Its powerful jaws clenched a 2 x 4; its thick tail slammed back and forth.

The guys tiptoed the reptile by Louie, whose throbbing head was recovering inside the fridge. Lincoln's hold was shaky, unaware he'd caught poison ivy in the woods. While I was considering the use of thyme, Linc suggested we remove the snapper's shell and use it as the cooking pot. Joey ignored him and hunted down a sixty-quart basin, big enough for the sea monster. I might have been the cook, but Joey was the boss.

Despite Lincoln's history lesson, that turtle topped the first Thanksgiving menu, the reptile's hissing scared the piss out of me. It would surely wake Shrimpy; we weren't going to pull this off. I convinced the guys to bring the animal back to the pond alive. The incarcerated can be so considerate.

RECIPE: GOOSEBERRY CRUMBLE PIE

1 (9") pie crust
2 cups of fresh or frozen gooseberries
1 cup sugar
1¼ cups flour
½ cup brown sugar
½ cup cold butter
2 tbsp. melted butter
½ tsp. nutmeg
pinch of sea salt

Preheat the oven to 325°F. Place the pie crust inside a round, 9" pan. Mix sugar, ½ cup of flour, melted butter, and nutmeg. Coax the berries inside the panned pie crust and cover with the sugar/nutmeg mixture. Place in the oven for twenty minutes and remove it from the heat. Prepare the crumble using the flour, melted butter, brown sugar, and sea salt. Knead the ingredients together. Twist into small pieces and lay out evenly over the top of the pie. Cook for twenty minutes or until a woody brown. Cooks up sweets for 6. *Optional:* marinate the berries in Grey Goose Vodka.

NEWS PAIRING: Force feeding geese to produce the delicacy Foie Gras is banned in sixteen countries and most US states.

71

CHAPTER 22

LET THEM EAT CAKE

I got a fan letter on the back of a prison menu.
I remember thinking, "They get pie. It's not so bad."
—Tina Fey

The Jewish pop opted for special meals prepared in Otisville's kosher kitchen. The kosher stuff was so highly regarded, Gentile inmates tried to fake their way into the program. (Fun food fact: Muslims can sue US jails for being denied halal rations.)

Our pokey was divided between Jews, Caucasians, Blacks, and Latinos. If you didn't fit into one of these groups, you didn't fit. Asian and handicapped, young Lin was doomed even before being ousted as a rat.

Lincoln and I picked up sanctioned ingredients for Semitic recipes in New Square. The haul was cottage cheese, tuna, canned baked beans, cereals, fresh fruit, and chocolate donuts. There were a lot of raised, Orthodox eyebrows in New Square when we showed up in matching greens, mandatory for cons on runs.

Linc's butt crack was exposed as he conversed with the butcher in slaughtered Yiddish. I thought the women's wigs would pop off. He swiped a meaty envelope off the counter and tucked it into his back pocket, pushing his pants down more than usual. Keeping it Clintonesque, I didn't ask and he didn't tell. We just quietly drove out of the holy hamlet.

Bobby baked up his best rice pudding, apple pie, and strawberry loaf cake, but with the limited amount of sugar the KCs gave him, his desserts were doomed. The scenario left the Gentile inmates bitter. I didn't care that the chosen ones got special sweets, I just wanted a choice, too. (Sugar was a viable drug here. A diabetic kid in my unit offed himself last year by guzzling a case of cream soda.)

Elon suggested I voice my complaints to Otisville's religious officer. After being put off for weeks, the relenting rabbi agreed, and "Cheesecake Friday" was born.

RECIPE: CHEESECAKE FRIDAY

32 oz. cream cheese

6 eggs

2 tsps. cornstarch

2 cups sugar

1 package graham crackers

1 pint sour cream

2 tablespoons butter

Heat the oven to 350°F. Line a springform pan with foil to the top. Crush crackers and melt butter. Place in the pan. Cook for 10 minutes. Beat cream cheese, eggs, cornstarch, and sugar until creamy. Fold in sour cream. Pour mixture into pan; bake for 70 minutes inside a larger pan filled with water. Cool and refrigerate. A religious experience for 12. *Optional:* top with Stonewall's raspberry sauce.

NEWS PAIRING: Murderer Rockne Newell sued a Pennsylvania jail claiming its high carb food made him moody. He demanded kosher meals in the future.

CHAPTER 23

AN APPLE A DAY KEEPS
NURSE BLACKIE AWAY

A gourmet who thinks of calories is like a tart who looks at her watch.
—James Beard

Prisoners are often portrayed as tattooed fiends who scarf fast food, chain smoke, and assault cellmates. Here's a helping of the truth: smoking is banned in jail, teens from Beverly Hills are inked up, and inmates seek out healthy feed. Supreme Court Justice Scalia noticed this, commenting that "many (internees) will undoubtedly be fine physical specimens who have developed intimidating muscles pumping iron in the prison gym."

In the play *Les Miserables*, Jean Valjean spends nineteen years incarcerated and is released more muscular than ever. In the film *American History X*, working out offers Edward Norton sanity. On *The Simpsons*, Homer assures Marge he'll be in better shape after his cartoon incarceration.

The Camp gym was a cylindrical hut that was always open. It housed a navy-issued machine that measured body fat. Bobby couldn't use it – he had metal parts in his peg leg – but his elephantine arms compensated for his missing limb. There were standard dumbbells, free weights, mats, and pull-up bars. Joey used a wide silver door hinge as a temp mirror.

Muscle mandates protein, which we got from tuna, egg whites, edible meat, and cottage cheese. Having muscles in jail was like sporting a suit of armor. Unlike some drug lords, we had no treadmills in our cells, but I was still addicted to working out. Bobby often said if we used our heads as much as our muscles, we'd be in better shape.

Creatine was key to locking down a beefy body, but the protein-based powder was contraband. Not a huge problem, just slip Lincoln some cash and he'd bag you a can of the popular white powder. It tasted like crap, but we'd tap it with orange juice and hit the gym running. Shrimp or shark in the brig – when you're healthy, you're wealthy.

On the occasional hot day, Sip would bring in a 16-ounce can of Del Monte fruit cocktail. Calories be damned, everyone looked forward to the sugar-soaked ambrosia she'd whisk together. The canned fruit cocktail stood in for fresh oranges, pineapples, and cherries. The marshmallows and shredded coconut came from the outside world. Her mix brought in color, festivity, even femininity. Nicky called her mélange "Food of the Gods."

RECIPE: SIP'S WORTH-THE-WEIGHT AMBROSIA

2 (16 oz.) cans of fruit cocktail
1 (8 oz.) package of shredded coconut
3 cups protein-rich yogurt
2 cups fruit-flavored mini marshmallows
1 tbsp. sugar

Drain the cans of fruit cocktail and place the contents in a large bowl. Fold in the mini marshmallows, sugar, and yogurt. Stir the mixture gently (don't work up a sweat) and refrigerate overnight. After a cool off period, top with the shredded coconut. Works out for 6 people. *Optional*: heavy cream can replace protein-rich yogurt if beefy bodies aren't your bag.

NEWS PAIRING: A study unearthed the fact that 75% of all plant-based protein powders test positive for toxic lead.

The prison-food was so bad, the inmates
decided to smuggle in a cordon bleu chef!

PART 4
ROASTING

CHAPTER 24

CAPTAIN CRUNCH

Sometimes the lamb slaughters the butcher.
—Amarillo Slim

Racial and religious cliques ate together, but there was an informant on the fringe of our Rat Pack. Travis never sang about anyone in the crew, so we stomached him. But he was a hardcore junk food junkie who caused a lot of wreckage. Lockers were often raided, with guards nabbing contraband. Grayson knew I'd use the foods later to make his meals, so I usually got mine back.

"BJ" was a captain in the Navy who was discharged for tossing an officer overboard. Lincoln said he looked like UFC fighter, BJ Penn; I thought he looked like a human pineapple with his bumpy skin, spiky hair, and oval-shaped body.

Travis's ship sailed when BJ decked him with a steel dumbbell for stealing and binging his Cheetos. The rat's orange, cheesepuffed mouth was now red with blood. Bobby despised snitches and proved it: he removed his fake leg and clubbed Travis with it, now on the floor looking like a twisted pretzel dipped in ketchup. Watching my co-chef use his limb as leverage was laughable.

After Indian guard Raj settled the scene, he prophesied we'd all starve in solitary. For Joey, damage consisted of a tousled head of hair, easily remedied with his folding comb that he held like a switchblade. Travis was taken to an outside hospital with a broken jaw and two black eyes. BJ was hit with an assault charge for using military force, and was transferred out of Otisville. This proved that even being a Captain in the clink doesn't prevent the system from sinking you.

RECIPE: BEETS BREAD

6 eggs
½ cup finely shredded sweet beets
½ cup whole wheat flour
½ cup apple sauce
½ tsp. vanilla extract
½ tsp. baking powder
½ cup melted butter

Preheat the oven to 350°F. Grease the sides and bottom of a 5x9 stainless steel loaf pan. Beat the hell out of the eggs and toss into a blender for two minutes with the rest of the ingredients (be sure the beets are fully smashed). Pour into the pan and bake for twenty-five minutes. The pink-colored bread is ready when a toothpick comes out unstained. Will be a hit for 3. *Optional:* top with Trappist Pineapple Preserves.

NEWS PAIRING: The red dye found in Flamin' Hot Cheetos can turn stool a bloody color. This has led to numerous panicked trips to US hospitals.

CHAPTER 25

THE OBESE ATE

I did thirty days in jail, got laid and drank beer.
—Vince Neil

The gym was a separate unit, a hundred yards from the Camp. It was open to every con, round-the-clock. Joey met Bobby and me to train after every breakfast and dinner.

During the end of a midnight workout, half a dozen guys from the black crew rolled in. They wore bright sneakers, swayed with confidence, and had a reputation for training out-of-shape inmates in exchange for commissary food.

Joey walked over to the leader with a smooth, collected gait. Bobby and I must have looked familiar from the kitchen, because one dude requested snacks from the mess hall. Bobby dropped his barbell to the floor and walked away tone deaf, making it clear he wasn't gonna lift a finger for anyone.

Joey circled back and asked me to grab food for the guys and their guests. The Enforcer taking orders? Fuck it, working out had made me hungry, too, and this sorry scene was getting heavy. Joey always knew what he was doing, and hadn't failed me yet, so I walked over the wet grass back to the main building for the grub.

Joey said the jailbirds were waiting on working girls; said we had to follow the Universal Code of Men and help our fellow felons get laid. So now I'm in the kitchen collecting cold cuts and crackers for this bunch of boobs. This was not a story I'd tell my grandkids: "Papa Phil picked out pickles, plums, and pastrami for hookers and hoodlums." I returned, arms full with finger foods, and laid eyes on The Hippo Parade.

I've got zero issue with big girls, but these babes were Barnum & Bailey material. Clowns never scared me this much. One was dressed head-to-toe in yellow; she looked like a lewd lemon squeezing through our penal window. Another's shiny maroon dress got stuck on the pane as she climbed in, reminding me of the curtains from The Billiard Club. A third fell right through, tittering and hitting her head on the concrete.

One looked painfully familiar. Joey confirmed it was the same frumpy, large lady that did the humping that day in the visitor's room. There was one blonde who was ample and even comely, but I was fairly certain it was a man.

Sex with any woman is welcome to most captives. Sure I wanted to . . . take a turn among the cabbage . . . but getting laid by any of these eight was a no-go. I dropped the goods I brought in and got the hell out. A lot of weight was tossed around that night.

RECIPE: MUSCLES X OCTOPUSSY SALAD

2 lbs. de-bearded mussels
1 lb. fingerling potatoes
1½-pound octopus
3 cloves garlic crushed
2 cups white wine
1 cup of Italian parsley
3 tbsp. butter
2 tbsp. fennel seeds
½ bunch cold asparagus
Olive oil

Remove the suckered arms of the octopus and wash well in cold water. Boil the soft-bodied tentacles in an oversized pot of salt water for 30 minutes. Drain, pat dry, and set aside. Sauté the garlic and butter in a large saucepan. Add the white wine, fennel seeds, and mussels. Cover for three minutes at a not-too-hot heat. Drain and set aside. Discard any undesirable mussels. Place the robust potatoes in boiling salt water for 20 minutes. When cool, cut into tiny, half-inch pieces.

Cut the octopus into ¼ pieces. Place them on skewers and brush fervently with olive oil. Cook on low heat, inside a window of two minutes, turning them over often. Remove the mussels from the shells and pair them with the potatoes and octopus. Sprinkle with olive oil, salt, parsley, and pepper. Garnish with eight long, cold asparagus spears. If desired, top with an easy lemon dressing. Lay this low fat, high flavor salad out for 6. *Optional:* pair with Spicy Hooker Trail mix.

NEWS PAIRING: A man was battered with a beer bottle after asking a prostitute if he could pay for sex with a boiled egg. The beaten buyer told the newspaper, "She could have just said no."

CHAPTER 26

THE HUNGER GAME

Sex… reminds us we're alive; it's the third most basic need after food and good movie popcorn.
—Billy Crystal

The library was in the admin building and housed a few hundred paperbacks and a handful of salty dime novels. Over the eight years at Camp, I read and reread my favorites books: *Concrete Blonde* by Michael Connelly, *Time Bomb* by Jonathan Kellerman, and *Coma* by Robin Cook.

The library was also the room where the white guys watched the tube. The black crews hung in the nearby "entertainment chalet," where the only VCR and workable microwave were outside of the living cubes. Known as "Code 21 Tower" and "Jerk-Off Junction," this was the place you'd nuke popcorn and watch any porn you'd get your hands on. The hut smelled like a Pussycat Theater, circa '76.

Raj was a security cop in the prison, but joyless "Chicken Pot Pie Monday" forced him down the hill once a week to the Camp. He'd meet up with Bobby and me for a tantalizing trade: mouthwatering porn tapes for makeshift tikka masala. We stuck cottage cheese in for yogurt, grinded chili flakes leftover from pizza night, and inserted ketchup as a substitute for tomatoes.

Raj was a physical and mental giant who always tried to shove prana down our throats. Not delicious Indian bread, but a Hindu belief that one's breath can replace food and water as a life force. I put that bag of goods out of my head.

On the inside, pornography was hidden in your mattress. Slice the bed open with the top of a metal can, and when the time comes, cover with bed linen and service one. On rare occasions, a guest could climb into the visitor's bathroom window and, with a willing buddy keeping watch outside, grease your loaf pan. Like summer camp.

An X-rated flick was the only thing Joey liked looking at more than himself. Jesus never watched—he preferred the company of real pussy-cats. Joey's favorite title was *PocaHotAss*, while I gave a raging thumbs-up to *She Came on the Bus*. I never understood the Fed's issue with porn. Wardens at Alcatraz had the right idea: using food or filth, keep the cons calm.

RECIPE: DEEP THROAT TISSERIE

1 (3½ pound) chicken
1 (14 oz. pkg.) Pepperidge Farm herb stuffing
1 pkg. sliced Portobello mushrooms
1 cup olive oil

Fowl rub:

½ cup olive oil
2 tsps. poultry seasoning
1 tsp. garlic powder
½ tsp. black pepper
½ tsp. onion powder

Preheat rotisserie to medium and thoroughly dry the chicken. Cook mushrooms in olive oil and mix into stuffing. Place mixture inside the bird and sew both ends closed. Drizzle on olive oil. Combine rub ingredients and entirely coat the chicken. Tie legs together and flip wings upward. Cook on a rotisserie for one hour, then deep fry in olive oil for ten minutes. Keep the meat... forkable. Place sticky, succulent fruits like mango and peach around the cock. Perks up 6.

NEWS PAIRING: @dany_hellz_kitchen is the popular Instagram feed of a French convict who conjures up food porn worthy delicacies behind bars.

CHAPTER 27

REVENGE IS A DISH...

Revenge is sweet and not fattening.
—Alfred Hitchcock

Nicky and Stavros were always psyched when their older brother, Harry visited. He'd drive up from Manhattan every other month to smuggle Greek delicacies in for the twins. When he'd arrive, The Greek Brothers would brazenly walk through the visitor's parking lot with the contraband in plain sight: pastries, garlic string beans, and lamb chops; more exotic, moussaka (beef and eggplant pie), grilled octopus, lakerda (salted bonito fish), and yemista (stuffed vegetables). I turned to jelly when galaktoboureko, hands down the world's best custard, came in.

Stavros would triple vex Bobby when he placed his two chrome serving trays in our walk-in fridge. Once, in retaliation, my co-cook used a salad fork to pick the lock on Louie's spice cabinet and dusted the Greek platters with nutty, hallucinogenic nutmeg (Billions served since 700 BCE). Bobby would blame the over spicing on his poor vision. In a nutshell, it was clearly revenge.

The brothers danced to a ghost orchestra far into the night. It wasn't lights out, but they were lit up, ripping off clothes, just totally out to lunch. Cons started to gather to gaze at these two nuts. Lock up Doc Elon watched, worried that the single tablespoon of nutmeg could shut down their hearts. Stavros might suffer a seizure; Nicky could drop dead from Sniffing Death Syndrome.

I pulled the duo off the invisible dance floor and got the giddy Greeks coffee'd up. Both of them had diarrhea for days. When Nicky found out what went down, I was relieved the knives were locked up.

Bobby's revenge mirrored my resentment and obsession with my snitch, Howie. I planned to stay on the warpath forever to avenge that backstabbing carrot top for turning on me. In prison, just having something to hold onto can be fulfilling.

RECIPE: GREEK UNDRESSING

2 cloves crushed garlic
¾ cup of Greek extra virgin olive oil
¼ cup red wine vinegar
¼ cup orange juice
1 tsp. Greek oregano
½ tsp. nutmeg

Whisk ingredients together, including the pair of crushed garlic cloves. Shake up before using. Not too much nutmeg! Use it on salad as a dressing, or on meat as a marinade. A knockout condiment for 4.

NEWS PAIRING: Malcolm X noted in his autobiography that "stirred into water, a penny matchbox full of nutmeg had the kick of three or four reefers."

CHAPTER 28

THE HILLS ARE ALIVE WITH THE SOUND OF FELONS

As life's pleasures go, food is second only to sex.
—Alan King

Eating in the mess hall doesn't differ much from enjoying a meal at the family dinner table; your day is discussed, future plans get set, and secrets are revealed.

Jesus was hangry, and kept eyeballing two middle-aged guys in the serving line who I recognized as fans of my oregano-rich meat sauce. The men, high on giddiness, were hatching something on the down low.

Post midnight count, on this balmy wet night, the dudes headed out for head in the hills. Seems their wives were waiting out of Camp bounds in the woods. (Bobby said the cooking oil was missing the next morning. I thought he was kidding.) Jesus caught them in time to demand pay-for-play: loot their ladies' panties, or give up the fun of night hiking forever.

Like men in lust, they couldn't keep their heads straight. They returned two hours later covered in muck, lingerie-less, hauling a bag of grub packed by the girls. They'd pay for defying The Mole. The next time they attempted to climb up to their orgy, Greta, Fury, and the Otisville SWAT team were waiting with open arms. The guys were charged with escape and immediately had five years added to their sentences. No more sticking their heads in the mud.

Despite what movies depict, escapes from prison are rare. Otisville once housed a man dumb enough to try. The collapsible barbed wire that made a ring around the institution sliced him up like a Thanksgiving turkey.

RECIPE: FOUR LAY-HER MUD PIE

8 ounces of Oreo cookies
8 ounces of Reddi-wip
1 package chocolate custard
1 pint fresh cherries
1 cup cold water
½ cup chopped walnuts or pecans
¼ cup sugar
2 tbsp. cranberry juice
2 tbsp. corn starch

Crush the Oreos and place in the bottom of a round dish. Freeze as the first layer. Top with nuts for the second sheet, and lay down a third layer of chocolate custard, and a fourth of Reddi-wip. Smother with warm cherry sauce.

For the cherry sauce: combine crushed cherries, sugar, and cranberry juice in a small saucepan at low heat. Whisk cornstarch into cold water until smooth and add the mixture to the pan. Bring to a boil and let simmer for 5 minutes. Stir until desired consistency is achieved. Satisfies 2 lucky couples.

NEWS PAIRING: Deputies in Dallas spotted an escapee on private land, hauling a duffel bag full of food. He was running back into the prison before sunrise when he was arrested.

CHAPTER 29

NEEDING DOUGH

Money poisons you when you've got it, and starves you when you haven't.
—D.H. Lawrence

In *The Shawshank Redemption*, elderly inmate Brooks Hatlen is released. He begins work at a supermarket, but cannot adapt. In a letter to his pals back at the prison, he finalizes, before his suicide, "Maybe I should get me a gun and rob the Foodway so they'd send me home."

My teenage cousin Frankie was a dead ringer for actor and murder suspect Robert "Baretta" Blake. Frankie didn't wear a cockatoo on his shoulder, just a big ass chip. Cuz got tons of attention from women, but turned everyone off with his deafening pity parties.

His criminal mind led him to serve thirty-five years for robbing convenience stores. Frankie was released once in the early 1990s, but he'd become so institutionalized he couldn't function in the tech-rich, changing world. His true home and family was with the cons up the river.

Frankie's lonely childhood was watered down with violence. It was an open secret he was the illegitimate kid of Aunt Connie and her pizza parlor-owning inamorato. This story turned him into a purebred liar and cheater.

The one time he was released, his freedom lasted four days. His downfall began with the sight of his first ATM. Like a diabetic salivating over a seven-layer cake, the beckoning machine was like a dream girl who only performed two functions: taking in – and spitting out – cash.

Frankie did what any ignorant, convict-in-love would do: kidnap a live teller after her shift and demand the dough from the automated teller. He was arrested that day, and sent back to jail until his early death, proving climbing the money tree can be fruitless.

RECIPE: KEEP COIN CAKE

6 oz. butter
2 eggs
1 extra egg yolk
1¼ cups flour
1 cup sugar
½ cup brandy or dark rum
½ cup orange juice
1 tsp. vanilla extract
¾ tsp. baking powder
¼ tsp. salt

Heat the oven to 350°F. Butter and lightly flour a Bundt pan. Allow your mixer to automatically cream the butter and sugar until fluffy. Steal in the yolk and eggs; continue beating. In another bowl, mix the remainder of ingredients until broken in. Now combine bowls and whip the loot smooth. Place mixture in pan and bake for 30 minutes. Let it cool off. Makes a money dessert for 6. *Optional:* drizzle Sticky Fingers Glaze over cake for a richer taste.

Feeling luckier than Frankie? After cooking the Greek-inspired cake, cool it, invert it, and place a coin, tightly wrapped in a 2x2" square of foil, into the bottom of the dessert. (Be sure to scrub the coin clean with hot soapy water or baking soda.) Grecians say the person who gets served the slice with the money will have good luck for a year.

NEWS PAIRING: Thieves in Manila smeared jackfruit sap onto metal cards and inserted them into ATMs. The liquid would stick to bills when customers tried to withdraw money, allowing the cons to later retrieve countless lots of cash.

CHAPTER 30

MEAT AND GREET

They found Carbone in the meat truck ... took them
two days to thaw him out for the autopsy.
—Goodfellas

Mob associate Tommy Milo was fined more than $3 million for US tax-related offenses during the 1990s. Milo was fat and frank, but fair (as long as he got his way). With his deep pockets and vast connections, he usually did. Another notorious inmate checked into Otisville at the same time as me: George Jung, the cocaine or "soda" king that Johnny Depp played in the movie, *Blow*.

I had no problem with Tommy's frequent requests for Sausage & Broccoli Rabe over ziti. His demands for the sausage to be cut into tiny pieces, and not to use less than six cloves of garlic never fazed me. I liked the jolly gangster. He was always good to me.

Tommy retained a lawyer to represent each of the garbage carting companies the government was forcing him to divest. That meant a different attorney visited Otisville Monday through Friday. Greta tried to block his extended visitations, but the judge overruled her sour ass.

The legal eagles always left their car trunks unlocked. Bobby and I would swoop in and unload pastries, Italian ices, and imported cigars. Treats for Tommy and his pen pals. Milo funneled the cash he scored back to me, and as one of the new town drivers, I'd buy food from an Italian pork store in nearby Middletown called The Salumeria. Getting found out meant a week in the SHU. It was worth it for the delicious delicacies, so I risked the ride alone.

The feast I fetched included calamari, pork roasts, fried pumpkin, beef braciole, shellfish salad, zuppa mussels, and stuffed porchetta. Mama Mia! The handmade strawberry cannoli made with sheep's milk was the mother lode – candied cherries and chopped chocolate folded into the ricotta filling. You'd never find this in the watered-down American versions, even at the top bakery on Hanover Street in the city.

From Christmas through New Year's, Attorney #1 made nightly deliveries to Milo. Not with French hens or turtle doves, although Joey would happily have cooked those. Rather, celebration trays of pasta (anelli, bucatini, orecchiette), fried fish (bronzini, fritto misto), vegetables (escarole, finocchio), and sweetbreads. Everyone topped off dinner with scrumptious Italian desserts like sfogliatelle (pastry) and baba au rhum (rum cake). Ten of us smashed into Tommy's cubicle for the holiday feasts. These were the best of nights.

One icy morning, Attorney #2 slid his cocoa brown Mercedes up behind the kitchen door. He was packing a dozen brick-sized filet mignons. I hid them in the back of the walk-in fridge, inside the pizza dough box, behind the canned peaches. My meat-obsessed mind forgot that Louie cooled off in the frickin' icebox after his cook. I thought it still unlikely he'd find them, but like a mutt, he had a sensational sniffer.

It was lost on Louie that the steaks were property of the crime boss he serviced on the sly. He forced Bobby and me to make lowly pepper steak with it for the inmates. Filet mignon pepper steak – the horror. Of course the cons loved it, except for Tommy, who heavily frowned on his stash being stolen.

Convinced I had outwitted the French fryer, I ran to retrieve the last two filets I had hyper-hidden under pounds of shredded carrots. Instead, I pulled out a pair of dirty, crusty socks with a Post-it Note stuck to them that read "Where's the beef?"

RECIPE: JUNK IN THE TRUNK SAUCE

1 lb. chopped beef
4 sliced large red potatoes
4 cloves chopped garlic
2 diced carrots
2 diced red peppers
1 diced red onion
1 can tomato sauce
¼ cup olive oil
½ lb. canned morel mushrooms

Cook the fat potatoe slices in water. Sauté the carrots, onion, and peppers in olive oil. Set aside. Puree the garlic and unload it into remaining olive oil. Add meat until brown and stewed. (Filet mignon works.) Add tomato sauce, potatoes, carrots, onions, peppers, and mushrooms. Simmer for an hour; bring in salt and pepper to taste. Dish over gourmet pasta noodles. Funnels in food for 4. *Optional*: add two tablespoons of red Ball Buster Wine to sneak in extra flavor.

NEWS PAIRING: Reversal of policy at the US Naval base in Guantanamo Bay, Cuba prevents attorneys from bringing in fast food or religious meals.

CHAPTER 31

A HANDFUL OF CHEATOS

Nine gamblers could not feed a single rooster.
—Yugoslav Proverb

Monday was pinochle night in the Camp. We played in quarterly matches without money; the draw was Mission grape soda, Keebler lemon cookies, and a bag of Cheetos. Oh the histrionics over five bucks worth of junk food.

My tournament partner was Lincoln, always a smooth talker but never a smooth walker: his pants crawled down his crack anytime he rushed between gigs. It vexed Teresa, but never Risa; wolf whistles and racial rants were folly for her fun.

Detainee Doc Elon and I held our cards in 'game signals' to dupe cons out of slop and stamps. Two fingers up? You're hungry for clubs. Three fingers? Go fishing for diamonds. Some things never change in or out of prison; cheating at cards is one of them.

Hustling Otisville's very own Nigerian Scammer was gratifying. He wasn't an urban myth from cyberspace, but a young bald, black man who smiled constantly. Nurse Blackie was a fan. Occasionally he would rip clusters of blackberries off the outside bushes and they'd stain his milky white teeth.

Pinochle was a warm-up for poker, always a full house on Saturday nights: Bobby, Nicky, Joey, Lincoln, The Nigerian Scammer, and not-invited but always-entitled, Jesus. Jesus's family ties to El Chapo were his instant invite to any game. He always had the most currency to play with, and rolled with trios of authentic, Atlantic City dice when we played Cee-Lo. (Without Jesus, dice were paper mached cubes of toilet paper, glue and water.) Binding commissary items like fiber laxative capsules covered most debts.

The heat turned up when hulky Raj was on duty. This cat was always spinning a tale. I secretly admired how he wrapped his long, straight hair into a man-bun. Teresa monitored the game from outside the room, wired to a walkie that was linked to the SWAT team. During play she'd search our cubes for contraband and confiscate my spicy Tatiana cigars. Smoking one of the rum and molasses-flavored beauties was like escaping to an internee's island paradise.

Jesus would try to throw everyone off during play by feeding chocolate to his white mouse, Maria (namesake of Spanish starlet, Maria Montez). Maria was not the sociable cutie from *Ratatouille*. She had too-big red eyes that looked like pomegranate seeds. She and Jesus were a compatible pair of creatures that turned deadly when provoked, and both were dirty rats.

The cartel kid never joked, especially when it came to playing poker for panties. He once ordered me to smuggle my daughter's dainties in to cover a four-buck spread. How I've imagined using my kitchen tongs to twist the strawberry mole off his face. Fortunately, six coveted cans of gas-reducing Beano that Bobby stashed away credited my losses; lingerie needed not be looted after all.

During one heartless summer game, Nicky accused The Mole of stealing a card. We all blew it off, but cold-blooded hothead Nicky lost it. He choked Jesus with one hand, and ripped his shirt and pants with the other. Maria got floored in the scuffle, along with the missing queen of diamonds.

Jesus got to his feet. He managed to cover his ass crack while mangling Nicky. Bobby tried to referee the fight between The Unholy Roller and The Enraged Greek, but it took The Nigerian Scammer to put the two on ice.

The match fizzled without Teresa (Risa), or Raj seeing a thing. But I caught sight of something sparkly poking out of Jesus' sweats: jeweled, showgirl-style undies. But What Happens in Otisville Stays in Otisville; I didn't dare undermine Jesus because of his past transgressions with intimates.

Late that night, Nicky became Lord of the Flies when Jesus basted the terrible twin in cooking grease stolen from the honeypot (a hole outside the Camp where lard went to die). The reeking Greek got locked overnight in the Camp maintenance closet.

Joey let him out in the morning, fearlessly joking that the oil would nourish Nicky's Mediterranean skin. A second fight ensued. Greta finally got her chance to switch on the hose and see if Jesus could walk on water.

Two weeks later, post-solitary, I saw Jesus in the dining room, crowned in oversized, metallic headphones, lost in his own world. I wondered what he was listening to. Every one of us sang a sad song in the slammer.

RECIPE: ARTICHOKE HEART CLUB SCAM-WICHES

8 oz. of sliced turkey breast
1 jar of drained artichoke hearts
1 can of sliced beets
1 head of romaine lettuce
1 package of goat cheese
1 package Chovi garlic dip
1 large loaf of Italian seeded bread
1 tbsp. capers

Cut the bread in half. Then cut each half lengthwise into thirds, creating two club sandwiches. Slather each layer with spades of garlic dip. Place lettuce on the bottom of each layer and deal up more sauce, sliced beets, artichoke, and a few capers. Spread mashed goat cheese on thick. Pile turkey in pillows onto the next layer by draping meat onto the bun, keeping the sandwich tall and together. Cut into diamond shapes to serve. Have colored, frill wood appetizer picks on hand. Rolls out lunch for 4. *Optional:* raise the game and break open a bottle of Ace of Spades Champagne.

NEWS PAIRING: Mobster Joe "The Boss" Masseria was found with a bloody playing card in his hand after being whacked at Nuova Villa Tammaro restaurant in Coney Island.

CHAPTER 32

DOCTOR IN-A-CAN

I could have a tumor… and they'd be like…
"I'd eat a tumor for the kinda money you're pulling down."
—Jim Carrey

The Camp housed two nice Jewish doctors. They were in for Medicare fraud. Like Elon, they'd dispense free council without bribe or braggadocio. This was unusual, since most lockup docs charge a rack full of ramen for a crumb of advice.

Stavros became disoriented one morning in the gym. When his speech changed – falling way below falsetto – I knew these were signs of a stroke; Dad suffered them at the end of his life. This Greek was not my cup of tea, but I already saved him once from OD'ing on nutmeg. Not helping again now seemed nuts.

Elon examined him, as Otisville doctors were slow and inept. He told the prison hospital director that Stavros immediately needed an outside infirmary. Nicky, raging that his brother could become a vegetable, rushed the ambulance that took away his twin a few hours later. Stavros would be fine, but Nicky would always be hysterical.

I had a walnut-sized boil on my back which was now starting to ooze like a boiling, cracked egg. It was just lunch's tomato soup staining the top of my uniform, but I told Louie it was my super-cyst leaking blood. I knew he'd throw me out of the kitchen and not care when I returned.

Teresa pushed to get authorization for me to see an outside medic, acutely aware it was actually blood. Despite the fact that the growth was starting to smell like death, Greta foreseeably disagreed with my need for care. The Nigerian Scammer offered to squeeze out the poison, but that was an email I could not afford to open.

Elon made the warden understand that my abscess would become *his* costly carbuncle. Chop-chop! At five o'clock in the morning, I was driven to the Catskill Regional Medical Center. My escorts were Grayson and some wannabe soldier. Grayson was sweating so much his ashy skin shined and gave off light in the rearview mirror.

The trooper held his TEC-9 pistol with an assault grip that assured me I was being driven to Rikers Island. Trying to make light of the situation, I leaned forward and asked Grayson if I'd be back in time to cook his dinner. All I got was a clammy nod.

General MacArthur sat outside my hospital room with his Uzi-like weapon drawn. A curious nurse asked him if I was dangerous. Since he didn't seem to speak, I answered from bed, "I'm not the one with the machine gun."

My joke wasn't any more successful than the lemon Jell-O they peddled, but the surgery was. I was holed up in my Otisville cube by afternoon.

RECIPE: CERISE & DECYST COCKTAIL

2 oz. yellow clotted cream
1 oz. vanilla vodka
1 oz. White Claw Hard Seltzer
½ oz. Chambord
1 blood orange

In a large blender, add the pungent liquors to two cups of cracked, shaved ice. Add the yellow clotted cream. Foam the liquids together with a hand frother. Operating gently, stir in the seltzer. Pour into a large cocktail glass and garnish with a slice 'n squeeze of the blood orange. A burst of flavor for 3. *Optional*: add an ounce of Nocello Walnut Liqueur for a taste explosion.

NEWS PAIRING: Aurum is a medical-themed eatery in Singapore where 'patients' enter through a morgue, dine at operating tables, and use cutlery from surgical drawers.

CHAPTER 33

BLOOD BATH

Kill no more pigeons than you can eat.
—Benjamin Franklin

The five-acre Camp lay at the bottom of a mountain that rose 1,500 feet to the prison. The area was a wooded playground for wild animals (sans the felons). Porcupines, cottontail rabbits, black bears, and red-headed woodpeckers gave the Camp grounds color.

Almost every afternoon, deer and raccoons would rush the kitchen door and wolf bread from our unsullied hands. Joey had no appetite for raccoon, and the deer could take him, so they were safe from the strapping sportsman.

The crew took advantage of the April morning and convened outside. Bobby pointed out a magnificent golden brown hawk racing through the sky (en route to execute a runty pigeon enjoying his last bird bath feet away). The squab's white wings made a scratchy, rustling sound as it barely escaped; then just a *thump* as it crashed into the Camp's admin window seconds later. The long-tailed hawk swooped in, snatched its bloody meal, and soared to the rooftop to lunch. Every one of us was hooked on the unsavory, Nat Geo sight.

The sun hit Grayson as he limped under the crime scene window. Then like a cake falling, he just collapsed, sighing one final groan on the baking hot pavement. Grayson had finished the race. He took the gold in my eyes, not because most of his teeth were capped that way, but because his devotion to God was the real deal, even in the face of Otisvillainy.

Bobby kissed his crucifix; Jesus seemed even-tempered as he lifted up the dead man's hand, but then heisted the jeweled football ring off his limp finger. I jumped to intercept the memento, but got hustled away by staff. They had started to crowd around the guard who worked at Otisville the longest, but had the shortest list of friends.

I looked for holy basil in the kitchen to tuck into his pocket. He said it was the best tonic for your mind, body, and soul. I couldn't find any, so I stayed inside and worked my aggressions out on the rolling pin. I'd pound out fresh bread for dinner.

A big bag of chocolate Easter eggs sat alone on the back of the counter. Grayson brought them in every Easter on his own dime. I chucked the rolling pin, and wolfed down every last one in good faith. I hoped Grayson had a bird's eye view of my sweet goodbye.

RECIPE: KILLING TWO BIRDS WITH ONE SCONE

2 eggs
2 cups flour
¾ cup cream
⅓ cup sugar
¼ cup dried cranberries
¼ cup dried cherries
¼ cup maple syrup
2 tbsp. shortening
4 tsp. baking powder
¾ tsp. salt

Heat the oven to 375°F. Rustle up an electric mixer to whip flour, salt, sugar, and baking powder together. Separately combine cranberries, cherries, cream, and one beaten egg to dry mixture. Stir well. Roll dough out on a surface bathed in flour and form into biscuit sizes. Feather the uncooked scones with the remaining egg. Cook in the oven until golden brown. Execute a sweeping of maple syrup before serving. Makes 8 scones on the fly. *Optional:* include Hawk Vittles Breakfast Casserole to allow your meal to runneth over.

NEWS PAIRING: 'Pigeon torture' in North Korea entails tying a prisoner's upper and lower limbs together and hanging him from the ceiling so he cannot feed himself for several bone-deforming days.

"The footprints in the cheesecake were inconclusive, but my DNA was all over the peanut butter pie."

PART 5
SERVED HOT

CHAPTER 34

PHILIP SCISSORHANDS

Once a guy pulled a knife on me.
I knew he wasn't a professional; it had butter on it.
—Rodney Dangerfield

Bobby and I were in the Camp kitchen preparing the French bread pizza and fries. I was using Sip's German knife, a dynamic piece of stainless steel with a curved blade that made it perfect for rocking back and forth to mince potatoes. This is what I was doing when Louie staggered in.

Louie absorbed the clattering of Bobby sharpening his foot-long knife heel-to-point, as I tossed slices of bread into the bubbling hot fryer. Oil splattered around, and Bobby and I cut up when Louie darted out of the kitchen like a frightened hare, pointing the long probe of a temperature sensor at us as he bolted out.

He had just demoted me after my green-collared crime of using oregano in the pasta sauce, so in his half-working mind, I was out to get him. It never crossed our minds the pussy went to fetch the police dog (and entire weaponized Otisville SWAT team).

Bobby got tossed to the ground on crutches. The huge blade he was working with tumbled to the floor, just missing his rubber-gloved hands. SWAT intercepted the knife and literally kicked me to the cookhouse curb. It took several officers to finally pin Bobby down.

We were face down on the ground for hours, knees in our backs and Fury's hideous breath in our faces. But it was Greta showing up that really made things stink. She felt so important, confiscating the "weapon" and locking it down with the other "armaments" in the kitchen cabinet. Now every knife would now be chained down every minute, only used with permission of a KC.

That night I had a dream about backstabber, Howie. *He comes to my house in Jersey while I'm having dinner with my wife. He lets loose that there's a dead girl in my apartment in the city and cackles. I become crazy anxious… deli meats and dishes fly off the table. Suddenly, I'm in my Manhattan apartment; a naked woman is snoring on the wet floor, next to a pile of cash and empty champagne magnums. Howie appears and starts taking advantage of her. I become furious and break his nose while loud metal music plays. He lets out another unglued laugh and licks the blood off his red beard.*

The dream was a true, bungled memory from six years earlier. Except in reality, when Howie licked the blood off his face, he threatened to kill me with a butcher's knife.

RECIPE: SWAT POTATOES WITH GIANT CHIVES

    4 medium sweet potatoes
    ½ cup milk
    ½ cup melted butter
    ¼ cup giant chives
    1 tsp. salt

Place the four skinned sweet potatoes in boiling, salted water. Cook for 25 minutes until tender. Using a sharp knife, cut off the woody ends. Slit in half and remove skins. Push potatoes face down in a bowl, adding butter and milk. Hard mash them, creating two cups. With a sharper stainless steel blade, slice off the stems from the long, rich chives and chop the leaves, throwing them into the potatoes for a faint onion flavor. A dreamy side for 3. *Optional*: for extra kick, add DASH seasoning blend to yams.

NEWS PAIRING: A four-hour standoff with a barricaded Florida man inspired a SWAT team to use a slice of Hungry Howie's Pizza to lure the assailant out.

CHAPTER 35

THE BLACKS, THE JEWS, AND THE STOLEN SHOES

"The time has come," the walrus said, "to talk of many things:
of shoes and ... cabbages and kings."
—Lewis Carroll

Half a dozen thugs regularly "broke it off" with the Otisville Jews. That is, they scared up money and merchandise from the Camp's chosen ones every Sabbath after supper. Within hours, any cash funds would get deposited into their leader's commissary account.

The head hood was a dark guy. He alone decided which of his minions would get a piece of the kosher pie (literally, as bites smuggled in by the Jewish bubbies were also poached). What a sight to see The Black Pack chowing down on latkes, kreplach, and noodle kugel.

The pack leader was a jumbo man who turned anyone in his way into human gumbo. The other hoods were hotheaded and young. We were hotheaded and ... older. Even The Greek Brothers gave the gritty Creole crew a pass, as fighting meant an invite up the hill to the big cage. Black, brown or white, no one had that appetite for destruction.

The Creole squad would get their kicks flaunting prison regalia: colorful Nike Air Jordans and Adidas Motombos, "gifts" friends of the Jews brought in to further appease the crooks. (Shoes are one thing, but when chocolate donuts were stolen off the Hebrew lunch trays, there was hell to pay.)

Teresa would always retrieve the sneakers and send the scroungers to solitary for a week. Pirating shoes from the Jews should have led to more time in the SHU, but we suspected the warden colored his decision in favor of his cons coming out of the mess clean. Quite a feat.

RECIPE: BLACKENED SOUL

3 fillets of sole
1 stick of butter
½ tsp. cumin
½ tsp. cayenne pepper
½ tsp. ground chili flakes
½ tsp. garlic powder
½ tsp. thyme
½ tsp. oregano
½ tsp. smoked paprika
½ tsp. onion powder

Mix the flavorful, dry ingredients into a rub and stick it to the fish. Do not use a heavy hand covering both sides. Butter up a frying pan and blacken the sole for three minutes before turning the fish over. Do not overcook. Remove from heat and lay down sour lemon wedges and tartar sauce. A shoo in to satisfy 3. *Optional:* a pinch of Double Bastard Hot Sauce spices up the seasoning.

NEWS PAIRING: Nike debuted a raw meat-inspired sneaker design that left vegans in horror.

CHAPTER 36

WAR & PIECE

An army marches on its stomach.
—Napoleon Bonaparte

Sip drove a rolling toaster (box truck) up the loopy hill every Monday to load reinforcements. As a former nun, she didn't have experience mastering a rig, but as a New Yorker, fuhgeddaboudit. On or off the wagon, she'd always get the job done. Just enlist Lincoln to pack up the meat, dairy, juices and boxes of raw vegetables.

With the goods came the bags of freeze-dried chicken. Three hundred squares of brown poultry jammed into a single metal container. They were literally pieces of history, eviscerated C-Rats leftover from the Korean War.

Bobby and I could work the roll of cooked bacon well enough, but there was diddley we could do to make the forty-year shelf life chicken chowable. He grilled, barbecued, braised and baked, while I spiced, seared and sautéed. Deep frying couldn't rescue the fowl. Even Fury turned her snout up to the slop.

Bobby knew the system sucked, but screwing him in the kitchen was crossing the line. He retaliated by flooding every crammed can with hot water and leaving them all outside the kitchen door for Jesus's felines to gut. A cat burglar who loved kitties. Purrfect.

RECIPE: DASHIN' KOREAN RATIONS

1 package dumpling wrappers
1 lb. ground pork
1 lb. napa cabbage
1 beaten egg
4 cloves of minced garlic
1 cup vegetable oil
⅓ cup soy sauce
1 tbsp. sesame oil
1 tbsp. sesame seeds
1 tsp. Korean red pepper flakes
1 tsp. minced ginger

Blanch the cabbage in water. Finely chop it to make it chowable. When cooled off, set aside. In a large bowl, work and mix all the ingredients, except the vegetable oil and water. Add the cabbage and mix again. Lay one of the dumpling wrappers onto a lightly-floured square work board. Place one tablespoon of the mixture in the middle. Moisten the edges with water and crimp to seal. Do not flood the dumpling. Master the process and repeat with remaining mixture.

In a large skillet, heat two tablespoons of vegetable oil. Place six dumplings in the skillet and brown on both sides for three minutes. Repeat with remaining mixture. When presenting, dip the dumplings in warm sesame oil. Yields 12 rations. *Optional*: add a lick of Fat Cat Chairman Meow's Revenge Hot Sauce.

NEWS PAIRING: Two women broke into an Asian restaurant and cooked their own food in cold water. After the drunk duo made off with a bag of dumplings, the NY restaurant's CEO said "While we can respect that one has cravings for our food late at night, it is still trespassing."

CHAPTER 37

ORANGE IS THE NEW CRACK

Health food may be good for the conscience, but Oreos taste … better.
—Robert Redford

Fifty pounds of carrots made soup and salad for a hundred inmates a week. Bobby said eating a bunch helped him sleep, but to me they were cherished, fibrous friends that kept my system rolling. Juicing carrots on the sly was a good substitute for sugary sodas, so we requested a dozen extra bags a month from the KCs. Joey made the heaps of pulp-evidence disappear, no questions asked.

Linc could carve a pot pipe out of an apple, but couldn't press a drop of calcium from a carrot. So Joey galloped to the plate with a smuggled-in commercial juicer, which we immediately stashed up in the ceiling tiles. The stud had his own stake in the juicing caper. He maintained that the brightest orange carrots made his black hair shiny. He also pointedly believed the stumpy tops were natural aphrodisiacs. I'd imagine Joey chomping on a carrot with one hand while whacking a guy with a gun in the other. Just like James Cagney munching and murdering in *White Heat.*

Always-late Sip was early today. Her beehive's tip-top form meant she was plugged in and sober. This made things sticky for us. We scurried to jam the juicer into the roofing while she reparked the truck. When

O'Mally entered, the widget's weighty cord dangled a foot above her head. If we could have just stashed it in her towering hive.

Bobby, Joey, and I sweated beta-carotene bullets as she took her time firing up lunch. It was inevitable she'd crack herself in the cranium with the plug. When it did finally happen, like a scene from Catholic school – a metal spoon in for a wooden ruler – she began to grill us. Who brought in the juicer? What was being blended on the down-low? Did we have a plan to trade the blade? Bobby said if we needed a weapon, we had plenty of tuna can tops. (My co-cook's frenetic personality always reminded me of Bugs Bunny.)

None of us found fried chicken on our plates that Sunday night, or the next Sunday. Tasteless cottage cheese and eggs – sunny-side down – were our spread. So much for using our noodles.

RECIPE: 14 CARROT GOLD JUICE

14 yellow carrots
6 ice cubes
2 oranges peeled, quartered
2 inches of ginger root
1 chopped mango
Cracked cinnamon

Peel the golden carrots and ginger. Place in a juicer, on a flat surface, with the fresh mangos and oranges. Bring out the ice cubes, add to mix, and blend all ingredients on high until creamy. Top with cracked cinnamon. Baits 3.

NEWS PAIRING: A man bit off his brother-in-law's finger during a brawl at Ditka's Steakhouse in Pittsburgh. The pressure used is the same force needed to bite a hefty carrot in half.

CHAPTER 38

TRUCK GESTOP

*Have I ever been tempted to break into Krispy Kreme
in the middle of the night? Oh, yeah.*
—Mike Huckabee

I relished my time alone on the stretch of highway "home" after I picked up the kosher foods from New Square. One morning at dawn, I watched a black bear drag her cub off the road in her mouth. This made me miss my daughter.

When I had enough cash, I'd spring for a one-pound bag of salt water taffy for the ride. The peanut butter, pear, and cinnamon flavors melted in my mouth. For a moment, I'd be a carefree kid at a carnival. Sadly, serenity came to an end before the highway did. Apparently a tip came in that contraband and cash were coming back to Otisville in my truck. This explained the security sedan blocking the entrance to the Camp.

The van's flashers lit up a young guard's flaxen hair in red and blue light. Fury's leash was wrapped tight to his wrist, rifle in tow. (Guessing his swastika arm band was at the cleaners.) Towhead signaled me to exit the truck. The way he held his M16 by the barrel confirmed he was not Otisville's cream of the crop.

His cerulean eyes looked black as skillets as he demanded to know what I was stashing. Who could think with the truck fumes nearly gassing me, and this kid tinkering with a loaded toy? I slowly exited the truck and truthfully explained that I never followed a manifest on kosher runs. I insisted I was only hauling the same special meals I picked up every week.

Full of piss and vinegar, the impubic guard directed me to unload every item off the truck. I did, but not before he beat an undefiled tub of kosher cream cheese to death. Food by food, box by box, the yellow-haired yutz trashed every pure provision on the ground, except two boxes of chocolate kosher donuts he helped himself to. An hour later, both animals stepped aside and I reloaded the vehicle with anything salvageable.

The same SS ("Sincerely Stupid") guard sent a Hebrew to the Hole the month before for refusing a breathalyzer test during Sabbath. It took one rabbi on the outside, and another religious officer on the inside, to convince the browbeater to let the perpetrator go.

RECIPE: GERMAN CHOCOLATE TAKE

3 eggs
3 oz. Kahlua
2½ cups flour
2 (9-inch) pans
1 package dark chocolate frosting
1½ cup milk
1½ cup sugar
1 cup butter
⅔ cup cocoa
1½ tsp. baking soda
1 tsp. salt
vegetable spray

Preheat the oven to 350°F. Beat the sugar and butter in a mixer until fluffy. Add the eggs and continue beating. Bring in every other ingredient and whip until mix is uniform and smooth. Pour into two, 9-inch sprayed, floured pans. Bake for 40 minutes. When cool, bunk one layer of cake atop the other and frost. Unloads dessert for 8. *Optional*: use a Food Guard lid to ensure the cake stays moist in any container.

NEWS PAIRING: A hangry Tampa Bay man was arrested after he flashed a .38-caliber revolver and fake police badge at Dunkin' Donuts to score a 10% discount.

CHAPTER 39

PUSS 'N BOOTS BUFFET

Titties and tater tots don't mix.
—Chris Rock

Lincoln and I could now ride together in the Camp's ramshackled Ford truck since I was also a Town Driver. He was thrilled to have some company and teach me the rural roads. I was upbeat just to get out of dodge.

Lincoln ran eatery errands for the KCs and gangsters. He also took appliances in for repair and dumped mattresses off at the junkyard for the big sleep. One horrendously humid afternoon, we hauled at least a dozen microwaves to town for service. The monotonous work and vile weather brought on vicious, unsuspecting Mac Attacks. I got lightheaded thinking of passing through the golden arches. My jaw tightened, foretasting the greasy feast.

We pulled into a nearby McDonald's (thirty miles off our approved route). I started to croon the old Mickey D's tune ("special sauce, lettuce, cheese, pickles, onions on a sesame seed bun"). We ordered, and I correctly pegged Linc for a strawberry shake man. We made it to the drive-thru window, when the server gave us the once-over and summoned her manager on the double. He peered at our prison greens and stack of beat up electronics. If Lincoln hadn't hauled us outta there like two hamburglars, we'd be dead meat.

Every Sunday, we'd bump along sixty miles of road to a Buddhist Monastery in Carmel, New York. The entrance was flanked by the largest

Buddha I ever cared to lay eyes on. We'd wait under the statue to pick up Bojo, an elderly, chain-smoking monk who prayed Sundays at Otisville. Sometimes he'd administer acupuncture to my shot right elbow from the back seat while cheerily puffing away on peppery, foreign cigarettes.

After we returned Bojo to the monastery in the late afternoon, we found ourselves with ninety minutes to kill. It just seemed practical…logical…to once and for all check out Puss 'N Boots strip club in nearby Newburgh. We always came upon the joint traveling through, but never made it inside. This new mouthwatering plan almost made me forget about the McDonald's mishap.

Just a few miles from Nirvana, we saw a painfully familiar figure, deftly changing a flat on the side of the road. B-u-z-z-k-i-l-l. Teresa was in a fix which left us in a pickle. The tire wasn't the only thing that deflated when we decided to pick her up. Damn it to hell – strippers seconds away! Our chance was utterly blown.

As we drove by the gentleman's club, Linc and I sulked like grounded kids passing the ice cream truck. Eyeing the establishment, Teresa acknowledged that Puss 'n Boots was the spot Louie called his "office." Then, leaving me more floored than seeing Joey with a five o'clock shadow, said we could stop for twenty as a thanks for picking her up.

Lincoln spun a hard 180. Teresa also changed gears, twisting the rearview mirror toward her and fingering her modest hair into quick, dirty-girl curls. Our distressed guard was morphing into randy Risa, right in front of our eyes. Parked, we jammed from the dirt parking lot to the muddy back entrance. The bouncer knew we were Otisville ousters by our clothing, and cock-blocked our way. But Risa nodded, and he moved aside. We were free to get our groove on.

Puss 'N Boots was small, but size didn't matter. The red leatherette bar blared music and hosted luscious ladies in thongs and matching cowboy boots. The buxom, buttered-up babes looked appetizing, but better than the self-service smorgasbord Lincoln gave love to a trough of pigs in a blanket, a rack of spare ribs, and two flaccid egg rolls before toying with the dancing dolls.

A blonde asked if I wanted a dance for a dollar. My brain rattled as the exotic "8" rubbed her backside against my frontal lobe. I scraped together one lucid thought: Stick with soda. Boozing meant a dirty drug test, time in the Shu, and losing my camp jobs. The "8" danced for me twice. She was three times a lady.

Linc flew into a private room with two "5"s and spent ten bucks. He was thrilled to finally get to drop his pants on purpose. Risa worked a lollipop when we left a few minutes later. I returned to the "office" one more time over the next seven years. When my pretty "8" retired, I settled for a strawberry blonde "7". She was distracting enough that I got the truck back late, and lost my gig as town driver. So much for my seat on the Otisville gravy train.

The only time I was ever driven to sexcessive behavior while cooped up was trucking to Puss 'N Boots for pay-for-play buffet.

RECIPE: STRIP STEAK X MONKFISH

2 (8 oz.) strip steaks
2 (6 oz.) monkfish fillets
1 lemon
1 cup Italian salad dressing
½ cup olive oil
1 tbsp. minced garlic
½ tsp. oregano

Souse the strip steaks overnight in olive oil, garlic, and oregano. Marinate the fish in the tangy salad dressing. Spread out the steaks and fish on the barbeque and stroke with marinades. Cook the red meat to desired temperature, pounding in coarse pepper and grinding in sea salt for taste. If it's flaky, it's ready. Lay the fish down with not-too-sour lemon wedges. Boots up food for 4. *Optional*: season with Sucklebusters Wild Thang Rub.

NEWS PAIRING: A five-month police investigation uncovered a Dayton, Ohio strip club that accepted food stamps as payment for lap dances and drugs.

CHAPTER 40

GREASE IS THE WORD

Leave the gun. Take the cannoli.
—The Godfather

Cannoli was in order, as family was visiting over the weekend. Bobby was a savvy, culinary con who managed to whip up the sweet and creamy ingredients for the filling, but making the tubes to form the shells? Recipe for disaster. We tried plopping the dough into the bubbling oil and shaping it over a short metal pipe we borrowed from the maintainance closest, but it was a plumb dumb idea.

Next, we wedged a wood rolling pin into the hinge of my locker door and broke off the ends. Seemed logical to create a tube shape. The dough just slid right off the floured roller, and cannonballed into the burning oil, stinging our skin like pissy bees. We resigned to serve the filling solo, in brown paper cups we took out of the dinner setups. Our concoction wasn't awful, especially after I ground up my own stash of pistachios and threw them into the mix.

Another unhappy ending: Louie found the contraband ricotta containers in the trash outside (why was he always in the garbage?) and punished Bobby and me with 6 a.m. "spill and burn" shifts working The Honey Pot.

The "HP" was an outdoor hole in the ground where ungodly cooking grease went to die. I'd have to succumb to half a dozen, fifty-foot jaunts from the kitchen to that noxious pit, but at least I had two working legs.

Making Bobby do it on a prosthetic? That stank worse than the greasy gorge Joey claimed "reeked like a thousand smashed assholes."

All the hauling and dumping meant a constant opening and closing of the heavy, bulky lid. You'd count yourself lucky if you got a whiff of any nearby apple tree. Finally, the enormous "Honey Truck" would roll in at the end of each month. Its automated suction tube would twist down the hole like an elephant's trunk, loudly snorting up all the raw, unfiltered lard.

Talk about living off the fat of the land: "Yellow Grease" is now the bee's knees of biodiesel fuel. Tens of millions of dollars worth is stolen from eateries every year.

RECIPE: HONEY POT PIE

1 (9") prepared pie crust
4 large sweet potatoes
2 eggs
1 cup sugar
1 cup honey
1 cup brown sugar
1 cup half and half
½ cup butter
2 tbsp. melted butter
1 tsp. vanilla

Preheat the oven to 350°. Boil 4 large sweet potatoes. Peel, mash, and mix in butter, preparing a total of 2 cups. Add sugar and eggs. Mix until smooth. Dump the batter into a crust that is holed up in an ungreased pie pan.

For Honey Caramel Sauce: mix sweet-smelling honey, brown sugar, half and half, and the melted butter in a saucepan. Stir the calorie-heavy concoction over a low heat; open and close the lid often to confirm the mix is thickening. Add vanilla; stir and remove from heat.

Pour the sauce evenly over the pie batter. Bake for one hour. Opens dessert up for 4. *Optional:* top with Musselman's Cinnamon Applesauce.

NEWS PAIRING: California Police rescued a would-be burglar after he was trapped inside a Chinese restaurant's grease vent for two days.

CHAPTER 41

THE CHEESE STANDS ALONE

Deadbeat dads are like a plague on society.
They should all be neutered with a rusty bread knife.
—Rotten Ecards

Otisville had a special facility a mile from the Camp and general pop. The Rat Unit was a totally isolated jail that had its own cook. I assume their food was the same as in the prison, but we had no contact with anyone there. It was a secretive lair, a den for snitches, ex-cops, pedophiles ("bacons") and inmates who feared for their lives. No one who checked into "The Polo Club" ever checked out.

It was the first day of Camp for a wealthy Hamptonite who forgot to give his kids lunch money for eight years. His effort to learn names and make friends made him look like the new guy at Camp Chipinaw in the Catskills. He didn't seem the least bit afraid or apprehensive as he took a seat next to the crew in the mess hall and asked for a tour. This new fish was gonna have trouble keeping his head above water.

Joey, Bobby, Lincoln, and I had just licked the last taste of pizza sauce from our pusses when the unprincipled parent lunged for the last slice. The drama began with Joey clamping down on the pizza with his right hand, and pulverizing a roll into crumbs in his left. Lincoln announced as town driver that he could permanently relocate any wiseguy anywhere.

Never-subtle Bobby twisted off his dummy leg and swung it over his shoulder like a baseball bat.

I got up and left disgusted, present in the pain that I wouldn't see my daughter for many years. Being her father was the only life sentence I would ever embrace. My Pop was no Ward Cleaver, but he'd burn furniture during the depression to keep his family warm. Our Brooklyn bathtub was often filled with eels that Dad fished from the ocean at dawn, so we'd have dinner by dusk.

The Coop Cafe made everyone vomit up their emotions. Our antics paved the way for the deadbeat dad to scurry down the road to hide out in The Rat Unit.

RECIPE: JERKY TURKEY

  1 boneless turkey breast
  ½ cup water
  ¼ cup soy sauce
  2 tbsp. brown sugar
  2 tbsp. chili garlic paste
  2 tsp. red pepper flakes

Isolate the turkey in the freezer for 30 minutes. Remove and thinly slice. Mix the remaining ingredients to create a rich marinade. Throw the sliced turkey directly into the mix. Cover and refrigerate for 24 hours. Heat the oven to 170°F. Drain and dry the strips before placing them directly on the oven rack. Keep an eye on the jerky by propping the oven door open with a nonflammable kitchen spoon. Cook for a minimum of 3 hours. Test if done by the taste; there should be no moisture present. Scares up 8 servings. *Optional:* make the meal money and pair with Loser Pale Ale Beer.

NEWS PAIRING: The comedy *Naked Gun 33⅓: The Final Insult* parodies inmate fights in prison mess halls.

CHAPTER 42

PEANUT BUTTER, POT, AND THE PRISON MYTH

People say you can abuse marijuana. You can abuse cheeseburgers, too.
—Joe Rogan

On the silver screen, drugs and prisoners go together like peanut butter and jelly. But in reality, "bug juice" is completely banned in the brig. Get busted buying or selling weed (trees), alcohol (hooch), or heroin (papers) and find yourself living the high life uphill in the max security prison.

When Indian guard Raj said we'd be subjects of drug tests in the morning, The Greek Brothers got colossal anxiety. Having been stoned the night before, and both being myth-minded, Stavros and Nicky decided I'd wave my magic cooking wand and conjure something up in the kitchen to turn their tests negative. If not, Greta would get a mouthful about the sex I shielded from her that day in the visitor's room.

I'm sure the Panama Red weed they scored from Jesus was just plain parsley and oregano. I didn't want to think about what was traded back and forth, since the buyers and seller detested each other. So I opened my invisible cookbook to the "Mighty Urban Legends" chapter, snapped my fingers, killed a few toads, and one recipe for the twins appeared: *2 cups peanut butter. 1 cup water. Eat. Drink.* Just call me The Icebox Wizard. Korean kids do hard labor to grow a single peanut, and we use handfuls of them to fake out prison pee tests. Shitty.

Greta and Fury sniffed out our cubes at 7 a.m. while Raj escorted each of us to the john. Four days later, the results were in. Was I smooth? Was my nutty spread bewitching? No, just the warden cleaning up another sticky situation to avoid tainting the Camp's reputation. We cooked up some clever coups in the can.

I'd cooked for burnouts in the joint before. A young pot dealer, Jake, was extremely ill, and pen food wasn't helping. So I prepared meat broth for the kid. Truth is, I spoon fed it to him twice. Grayson used to say "Only the pure of heart can make a good soup." Was there hope for me?

One blistering midnight, Jake asked for a rare steak. Sure, and I added a sweet marinade mixing Coca-Cola and mustard. But he was past all that. The medics came for him with a stretcher in the dead of night, and he died the next day.

RECIPE: DOPE PRISON BARS

3 egg yolks
2 (16 oz.) packages of cookie dough
1 can sweetened condensed milk
½ cup creamy peanut butter
½ cup finely chopped walnuts
¼ cup peanut butter-filled pretzels
1 tsp. vanilla
vegetable spray

Heat the oven to high, or 350°F. Cover a 13 x 9" pan with vegetable spray. Smash the pretzels. Dispense the cookie dough evenly in the pan. Cook for 20 minutes or until golden brown. Remove from the oven. Mix the remainder of the ingredients together until smooth, and spread evenly over the pan. Cook for an additional 25 minutes. 24 bars will be baked.

For marijuana bars: melt ⅛ cup of salted cannabis butter over low heat. Add ⅛–¼ ounce finely ground legal marijuana to the pot. Stir often. Simmer 4(20) minutes. Lower heat for another 25 minutes. Strain. Add to the dough before it gets cooked.

NEWS PAIRING: Alabama inmates smeared peanut butter over their cell block number, confusing guards who opened the door and aided in their escape.

"*Shishito peppers really are everywhere now.*"

PART 6
BON APPETIT

CHAPTER 43
HUG-A-THUG

It was Christmas in prison and the food was real good…
we had turkey and pistols carved out of wood.
—John Prine

I smuggled chicken drippings out of the kitchen for Charlie in the next living cube for years. Finally, he offered me up some of his Thanksgiving ramen. His milk-and-water gravy, canned peas, and industrialized instant potatoes were proof that holidays in The Hole lacked heart, but I did appreciate his offer. Otisville KCs put out a turkey loaf, and you ate it, grateful if Sip did the cooking that year.

Christmas was no jollier, unless you counted Chief Pontiac's tricked-out tuna cans hanging in his cell as ornaments. A sweet punch spiked with 7 Up was lapped up by most, but I turned down the gift of guzzling sugar. Grayson would at least holler up hymns during holiday patrol, but now, ne'er a peppermint bark in sight.

I made my daughter a candy wreath every December. Constructing it for her was worth twelve days of paper cuts. The Christmas sweet-meat-treat looked and smelled like love to me. My Grandnana taught mom, mom taught my sister, and Anita showed me one night watching *American Bandstand* on our rump roast-sized TV.

The wrapped candies I used were commissary fare: green striped peppermints, round yellow butterscotch drops, and red cinnamon drops. The pink watermelon and purple grape Jolly Ranchers added color. (My daughter was truly an attorney-in-the-making, petitioning me to remove the too-hot red cinnamon drops.)

Colored kitchen string made tinsel. I composed the wreath's ring by twisting aluminum foil around a circle of reinforced plastic spoons. The kitchen's egg ring would have worked nicely to back a small one, but I wanted to send the very biggest bundle.

Campers were to be assembled in the dining room at 4:00 p.m. on Christmas Eve. The Italian Stallion's hands and face beamed holiday orange after another vain, saffronic attempt to self-tan. Anyone with horse sense knew not to say neigh to Joey.

Mutts Fury and Greta, Nurse Blackie, Raj, and Louie all showed up to shepherd staff. Bobby, Chief Pontiac, Jesus, Lincoln, The Greek Brothers, Joey, Elon, Lin, and the ever-merry Nigerian Scammer were all present for the annual 'Hug-A-Thug' event. No, nobody took us in their arms; gifts were hearty handshakes from the warden.

Sip was cloaked in Christmas green, and was hauling her sugary, Irish ambrosia on a glass tray with brass handles that brought some class to the bash. Even Fury was in good humor, licking frosting off the floor. Greta managed to look grave, even in the oversized pearl earrings and brooch that made jewel-loving Jesus drool. Louie spent all his time polishing Warden Keyes' apple, but this afternoon he had fierce competition from Nurse Blackie; she was feeding the boss the rhubarb pie no one else wanted to eat. Crappy Holidays.

It was Risa's arrival that put the "mas" in X-mas: gold foil braided into her hair, Santa-sized cleavage, and shiny red lips. Her too-sweet cologne flashed me back to the tall blonde I lusted after at The Billiard Club. Louie wolfed around her, but she wasn't one to get her tinsel in a tangle. Fury jumped on her hind legs to scratch and sniff Christmas Barbie. That was the sole smile I cracked that day.

I left early and roasted chestnuts on an open fire. (Fine, I went back to my cube and cracked warm peanuts heated in the microwave.) As I was walking out, Risa snuck up behind me and thrust a wooden box under my arm. It was filled with the rum-flavored cigars Teresa nabbed on countless locker searches.

I brushed the nuts off me, left my pity party, and went out to the tennis court. I lit a cigar up in honor of my time going by.

RECIPE: ISN'T HE A PEACH? SHAKE

4 fresh peaches
4 cups vanilla ice cream
1 lime
1 tray of ice cubes
1 package Christmas holiday sprinkles
1½ cups milk
½ cup peach-flavored vodka
2 tsp. vanilla extract

Squeeze the lime. Allow the juice to hug the edges of four large glasses. Pour the holiday sprinkles onto a small plate. Turn the juice-rimmed glasses down to season the edges with the Christmas candies. Place in the freezer until frosty. Gather the peaches together; peel and slice them, then blend with remaining ingredients, including vodka if desired, until smooth. Pour into the cold, candied cups. Sleighs 4.

NEWS PAIRING: Angry at her mother for taking her iPhone, a twelve-year-old attempted to poison her parent – twice – by blending bleach into mom's health shake.

CHAPTER 44

THE SPANIARD AND THE SNITCH

They eat us hungrily, and when they are full, they belch us.
—William Shakespeare

Looting the kitchen was one of Jesus' many transgressions. Tomatoes, tapioca pudding, utensils—he took what he wanted, and I felt forced to cover for him when the KCs inquired.

Jesus's efforts to corner the Otisville orange juice market already got me axed from my kitchen job. I was sour, but said squat. But, when he made a move for my breasts, I decided to bust him. I was entitled to two cuts of every bird I roasted for inmates, and no one was going to make me look like a boob.

I told my trusted friend Bobby about my play to spill the beans on the Spaniard. I was angry and blowing off steam. The longer the KCs took to meet me, the more I waffled about ratting. No matter; gossip was gospel in the pen. With a wave of an apron, I turned into an ostracized informant, or in slammer-slang, a "chocolate frog."

Someone else had ratted out The Mole's kitchen sins, but I was targeted to take the blame. Snitches get stitches, but I died a different death. Outside of Lincoln, I was cast out by the crew who promised to honor, defend, and like me. But like it's said, "Promises and pie crusts are made to be broken."

Bobby and I sautéed in silence from then on. Joey turned to ice and changed cubes. I tolerated unending, squeaky rat sounds from The Greek Brothers when I walked by. I never needed to look for a knife again, as there'd always be one in my back.

It was no clambake living at Otisville now. More and more, I'd hole up alone in the kitchen. Once, after a deafening game of solitaire, I saw Jesus. He was alone at the large dining table wearing his gold headphones and savoring a sloppy PB&J. This would be the first time we were alone since the half-baked bull I was an informant.

I prayed he'd eat and run, but he eyeballed me, approached, and sniffed me over like a vulture querying a carcass. His strawberry mole raisin'ed up; his mouth shift-shaped into an ireful frown. And then he looked at me dead in the eye. Was there more to the cartel cousin than cards, cats, and candy?

I could feel Jesus inside my head, twinning in the idea that our pride, desperation, and depression weren't hidden, but raging on the inside. Both of us longed to find some complicated person or adrenaline-fused situation to fill up on and distract us from our sad truths. Outside of me not having color moles or chiseled cheekbones, and being privy to wearing men's underwear, it was a sad sack of truth: we were Italian-Mexican peas in a pod. He knew I was no rat.

Jesus backed down and perched himself up on the dining chair to savage the rest of his sandwich. I headed back into the kitchen, giving myself permission to once again breathe. I grabbed a jar of chunky, strawberry jelly – the good, local stuff – and rigged us half a dozen PB&J sandwiches to smooth things out. I hoped the Spanish proverb "The belly rules the mind" would ring true. I didn't give a jar of jam anymore whose panties he was hiding in. I sat down, we broke bread, and silently made peace.

Acting distracted by the peanut butter stuck to the roof of his mouth, he shimmied off Grayson's football ring and surrendered it. We were cool. I'd gut out the short time I had left at Otisville with Jesus on my side.

RECIPE: OSTRICH-IZED ENCHILADAS

1 lb. ground ostrich meat
3 sliced jalapeño peppers
3 tbsp. olive oil
2 cups crumbled Mexican cheese
1 can spicy enchilada sauce
1 can black bean salsa
1 package corn tortillas

Preheat the oven to 350°F. Rig up a baking pan and coat with vegetable spray. Look over the ostrich meat as you brown it in a skillet so it doesn't get burned. Transfer meat to a bowl. Add ¼ cup of enchilada sauce, salsa, and half of the Mexican cheese to the meat. Fill up tortillas one-by-one with the mix. Close the enchiladas – which are all now alike – and place seam side down in the pan, nestled together. Pour hot olive oil over them and top with remaining cheese, sauce, and peppers. Cover with foil; cook for 45 minutes or until sauce bubbles. Fills up 3.

NEWS PAIRING: *The Washington Post* reported that Anne Frank was likely betrayed in hiding due to fraudulent ration coupons, not as trade for half a loaf of bread, as widely reported.

CHAPTER 45

THE TURNOVER

… and then my poor meatball rolled right out the door…
—Children's rhyme

As vice president of a bank, I learned about loan sharks. As a business owner, I had to swallow snarky bankers. But the motley crew I braved at Otisville took the cake.

Joey was sent to a Boston brig after some hot-headed horseplay. Whether he snuck in hair dye, used a mirror as a weapon, or fried up another goose pie, no doubt his fate was sealed by Greta, who clawed her way up the cooler's corporate ladder. This stud could never be corralled, and I pitied the fool who meddled with the meticulous mobster who helped me stomach 3,500 days in the joint.

Linc had big plans. He returned to the UK and launched a limo service. For ten years, we stewed in shit together at Otisville, and yet our madcap adventures left a sweet taste in my mouth. Would his business and customers satisfy his constant craving for company? All these different, daring men – big hearted, small minded, Muslim, Mexican, even the guards—everyone suffered epic loneliness in jail.

Bobby was no longer my boon companion, cohort in kitchen crime, or friend. Yet I would miss the marvelous, peg-legged cynic. His wit and sarcasm always inspired food for thought. Wherever Nicky and Stavros landed, I'm sure it was on the water, as fish everywhere had it out for them.

Jesus was sent to solitary for ninety days the weekend after I left. His appetite for Sip's emerald ring became voracious, and he clumsily stashed the spinach-colored sparkler in Maria's ratty bed. The King of Jewels would always hunger for a fast fix. Had I lost my taste for the Insta-fix? Or would I make a mess of things all over again on the outside?

The lights went out for my Muslim princess after September 11th, proving that even nonviolent Camps like Otisville can snuff out sympathetic spirits. Did racial rants cause Teresa intolerable depression? Did Risa's fire burn her out? Was her lack of joy unlivable? Whatever her recipe for destruction, I remained fearful she had poisoned herself with fare from the prison kitchen.

Louie left Otisville after 9/11 and started a restaurant with an excon in the Cayman Islands. I could picture the willful grifter, sweating straight into the fresh Caribbean seafood. His enterprise didn't float, and when he tried to swing another Kitchen Cop job at Otisville, he was rapidly rejected.

My "last meal" at Otisville was a can of cooked salmon which I ate alone on the tennis court with no chums around. Zero-love.

Just the inescapable, twisted fates of a bunch of meatballs with nothing but thyme.

RECIPE: MEATBALL MEDLEY

3 cloves sliced garlic
¾ lb. ground chop meat
¾ lb. ground pork
1 cup breadcrumbs
1 egg
½ cup grated parmesan cheese
¼ cup toasted pine nuts
¼ cup golden raisins
¼ cup mozzarella
2 tsp. oregano
1 tsp. basil

The oven must be preheated to 350°F or the recipe will fail. Group the meats, breadcrumbs, spices, garlic, egg, parmesan cheese and stir them all together. Separate the mixture into three equal parts, shaping each into the size of large golf balls. Knead extra, varying ingredients into medleys: pine nuts to the middle of the first third, raisins to the middle of the second, and mozzarella to the center of the last. Spray a baking tin and place the different eatables together on it. Make a plan to bake for ten minutes on both sides. Makes memorable meatballs for 3. *Optional:* add La Famiglia Del Grosso sauce on top before baking.

NEWS PAIRING: A Denver resident left a sign in his yard threatening to feed poisoned meatballs to his neighbor's dogs if the pups pooped on his lawn.

CHAPTER 46

WRAPPING IT UP TO-GO

Welcome to the Gunshine State.
—DJ Smallz

As my sentence neared completion, I was given the option to move into a halfway house to smooth my transition back into society. I was allowed to settle near my mother and sister, so for the last six months of my penance I was a freeman in West Palm Beach, Florida. I arrived with a lot of baggage.

Lincoln had become the closest friend I had ever made, and I felt a flood of sadness parting waves. I think he'd miss my white ass too, because he took the trouble to get me three Big Macs, the burgers that got away that day hauling – and getting – ass in Newburgh.

Lincoln chauffeured me to the bus station in a bowtie, as I devoured Mickey D's like a dude still on-the-run. Linc's Big Mac move moved me, and when I got out, I hugged him – hard. Then I slapped him on the back and made a dumb joke. Two macho men saying goodbye.

When I left Otisville in 2001, the world had radically changed. People were talking to cell phones instead of to each other; water was bottled and sealed for security, and a cup of coffee had become the bastard cousin to "cold brew." Fast food restaurants were now on every corner in Florida, but mini-marts were jammed with fat-free snacks. Waitresses were now waiters, waiters were called servers, and servers who made a pot of joe were christened Baristas.

I felt numb unpacking my bag, until I reached down to the bottom of my duffle and got sliced with a paper cut. The sting wore off when a sausage-thick bundle of twenties inside an envelope caught my eye. My ex-cubemate, the handsome hitman and chef extraordinaire, left the dough and a number of a pal who owned a Palm Beach chophouse. He also left a short note: "Ciao."

My Otisville locker was traded up for a wood armoire at the halfway house. Cotton towels replaced the scratchy, polyester ones my skin had grown used to, and I used a toaster for the first time in ten years. I slurped and slurped coffee with copious amounts of caffeine, and snacked and snacked while reading the newspaper in the cozy cardroom.

The first local story I read involved a Wendy's customer hurling a four-foot crocodile into a drive-thru window. I'd imagined Florida as a sunny, sexy place, but it was really just a haven for discarded people. Sunken treasure aside, something was in the water here besides alligators.

I was forced to find a job immediately, or risk returning to Otisville as a bad egg. The Chop House wasn't going to work out because of the distance, but I landed a nine-to-fiver at the local market, Publix. A quarter of my earnings went to room and board, a fact I couldn't control any more than being assigned to the deli section in the far rear of the store. The upside? I was being probed by a peroxide-pretty who worked in the dessert section.

Brittney wore white cowboy boots and a denim skirt everyday under her green Publix apron. I felt like "Silly Philly" again, having no idea what to say to her. But she took the lead, offering to trade cheesecake for chicken on the sly. I came to look forward to the hand off. (Brittney's smoker's laugh reminded me of Nurse Blackie, who I never saw again after the Christmas party. I hoped she hadn't tried to give herself a shot.)

Brittney would dish up unsound stories about Publix: a woman arrested for potato salad rage, a ninety-year-old man charged with assault for hurling a watermelon at his caretaker, and a couple who weaponized cottage cheese against each other in the dairy section. Stories of Brittney's husband using his lunch truck to stage car accidents were equally mental.

I must say, she did bring some human feelings back, but she was married, and I didn't need that baloney.

The halfway house cafeteria was a complete change with its white wooden chairs and stainless steel silverware. Publix donated food to the house like egg, tuna, and chicken salad sandwiches (and ghastly veggie wraps). Desserts were fruit pies, butter muffins, and glazed banana cake, all of which I heartily approved of.

Dinner was usually a chicken breast that would start out skinless on Monday, and be parmesan'd with layers of sauce and cheese by Friday. Fortunately, my mother and sister drove up every other weekend with homemade meals like roasted potatoes, meatloaf, and sausage soused in Mom's homegrown basil. Mom's apricot cheesecake was still so fresh when it got to me that the creamy top layer jiggled.

Three sisters, who I called The Bitches of Eastwick, ran the "Haus." They lacked taste and patience, and thrived three times over on pettiness and punishment. Bewitching they were not: they'd boil every con in a cauldron if they could. I had to empty all the trash cans for two weeks because I rented a tape from Blockbuster without their spell of approval.

The administrator, Nina, was a hoary Spanish woman that prayed more than Grayson. She looked harmless in black lace and a huge bun of white hair (I always thought it looked like a powdered donut). But Nina was a wicked tough cookie. She didn't hire security guards; one of the sisters by the front door with an invisible sack of cloves was enough to ward off trouble.

I befriended a tenant named Stan, who belonged to the notorious Outlaw Motorcycle Gang. He had worked as a kidnapper for the Mafia, but his job now was washing dishes. He had a winning combination of Bobby's edge and Joey's charisma. He twiddled his untamed beard like Joey twisted his chevron mustache when cooking up a plan.

Stan said The Outlaw Club controlled most of the strip joints in South Florida. He'd invite me to visit the scene, but a quickie in this new world felt more lethal than kissing an anaconda. Maybe I just wanted affection. Anything's possible. Or was my bang-up time at Puss 'n Boots with Lincoln and Teresa unmatchable?

I was stunned when two redheads (I don't think they were from the church across the street) delivered him a new, blue Harley. More so that the witches let him keep it (maybe they thought it was a fancy broom?). Stan polished "Fat Boy" in small circles, round-the-clock. He revved it up one sunny Palm Beach morning while neighbors bitched and barbecued from their front lawns.

My family and I were playing pinochle on the porch, when this unmarred day was totaled by gunfire. Mangos and avocados from the outdoor serving table bombed my mother and sister as they hit the cement to hide under the umbrella tables. Fruit exploded under people's feet as they darted around in every direction. The addicts next door in the rehab center finally got the adrenaline fix they longed for, with cops and cons bellowing and bustling about.

The drive-by target was Stan. He steered clear of the flying lead, but Fat Boy wasn't so lucky. The sea-colored chopper was shot to hell—tires busted, paint blasted, pipes slivered and shattered. Turns out the hit was payback for Stan kidnapping the wrong woman. Seems my Floridian friend mistook a mob boss's daughter for his intended she-target.

I had bunked with a mademan, cooked for a crime boss, buddied up with a hitman, and done a million-dollar drug deal. It wasn't until I got to the Sunshine State that things really started to melt down. You'd think time in the Haus wouldn't be half bad, but it was really three times a bitch.

RECIPE: TROLL HAUS COOKIES

4 cups flour
2 eggs
1½ cups butter
1½ cups white and brown sugar
1 cup chopped nuts
½ cup white chocolate morsels
½ cup dark chocolate morsels
1 tsp. baking powder
1 tsp. baking soda
1 tsp. vanilla extract

Preheat the oven to 375°F. Mix flour, baking powder and baking soda in a bowl. Separately cycle in butter, white sugar, eggs, and vanilla together until you stir up a creamy mix. Halfway through add in nuts, dark chocolate morsels and sister white chocolate morsels. Combine with flour mixture. Conjure into 1½-inch squares. Place cookies length apart on a floured, metal sheet. Bake for 12 minutes or until golden brown. Shoot for 40 cookies.

NEWS PAIRING: Crops of infected rye may have caused the "possessed" behavior of women labeled Salem Witches in 1692.

CHAPTER 47

REGRITS?

After a good dinner one can forgive anybody, even one's own relations.
—Oscar Wilde

There were no walls between my mother, sister and me when they came to the Haus for my release. Both were genuinely warm and sunny during the drive home to Deerfield Beach. I wasn't returning any war hero, but I had been missing in action for ten years. It felt stupendous to be welcomed back by family.

My sister Anita baked the anisette biscuits I used to dunk in milk after grade school. She laughed and cried as I devoured the priceless treats in the backseat. A tin of her handwritten recipes she gifted me popped in my mind. I hadn't thought about that box or my birthday in years. Her honey almond grits took over my mind. Then her sesame cookies. Clearly, I was getting my senses and appetite back, but I didn't want to ask anything more of my sweet and selfless sibling.

I hadn't cried since my younger brother, Ross, died of kidney failure fifty years ago, but I guess even the manliest of men spring a well every half a century. That night I let it out stockade style: in the dead of night, alone in the bathroom, towel over my mouth, without a peep.

I slept until noon the next morning. I would have remained comatose, if not for the smell of Mom preparing eggplant parmigiana, a recipe passed down by Grandnana in the 1800s. Nana did not fuck around when it came to food. She served a whole roasted lamb's head on Easter once when I was five. I'm not sure I've yet to recover.

Mom tackled Egg Parm better than Bobby or Joey. She wasn't as messy as those characters, and far more patient. She'd grate cups and cups of fontina, provolone, and parmesan cheese. I once asked how she knew how much to use, since the numbers were worn off her glass measuring cup. She'd smile at me, and continue to roll hand-cut breadcrumbs in minced garlic. Our language of love was food.

Gilda laid down law and order when it came to cooking: cut eggplant slices extra thin, fry only two pieces at a time, and brush vegetables with olive oil – never pour it into the pan. The soaking of the eggplant in milk to cut the bitterness was key. (Should I soak in milk?) I watched the cheese bubble through the glass oven door that afternoon like a kid, and gobbled the magnificent meal for days.

My family's generosity made me feel crummy. The shame was sharp; I felt it in the pit of my stomach. Was it being a decade older, spending ten in the pen, or all that carrot juice that helped me see what a Grade A asshole I'd been? My mouth tasted like crow.

My ex Sheila never visited, called, or wrote me in jail. This was probably because I was a chickenshit husband who blamed her for my distasteful choices and insecurities. It was becoming clear that my own appetite for destruction landed me behind bars.

That night, for the first time maybe ever, I prayed that jail's sobering affect would not go down the drain. Grayson turned out to be right all along. In the end, it would come down to a mustard seed of faith to see me though.

The next day, Anita surprised me with a dozen sesame cookies for each year I was away. That's a lot of dough. She made them with the softest butter and unhulled sesame seeds. Their rich aftertaste planted a hopeful feeling in me, and even a plenteous thought: If Howie hadn't cut my days as a drug dealer short, I may have spent my entire life on ice. Maybe I even owed him a rotund 'Thank You' for setting me up.

RECIPE: SIS'S SESAME SENSATIONS

4 cups flour
2 sticks softened butter
2 large eggs (room temperature)
2 cups unhulled sesame seeds
1 cup sugar
½ cup whole milk
1½ tbsp. baking powder
1 tsp. vanilla extract
½ tsp. salt
½ tsp. orange zest
½ tsp. of lemon zest

Preheat the oven to 375°F. Cut up butter into pieces. Generously butter and flour two sister cookie sheets. In an electric mixing bowl, stir up flour, baking powder, and salt. Now work at a lower speed, gradually add the butter. Whisk eggs and vanilla in a separate bowl. Add in the orange and lemon zest to make the flavor memorable. Bring the egg mixture into the dry ingredients until all is smoothed over.

Place milk in a not-too-shallow bowl and spread sesame seeds on a family dinner plate. Shape dough balls about 2½" x ¾". Lovingly roll cookies in milk, then the seeds. Place one-inch apart on the two cooking sheets and bake for 25 minutes or until browned. Gifts 30 cookies. Thanks, Sis.

NEWS PAIRING: A Florida man used a butter knife to open the door of a mobile home. He told police he broke in to get sesame seeds for his hamburger.

CHAPTER 48

THAT'S THE WAY THE COOKIE CRUMBLES

Bad taste leads to crime.
—Katherine Hall Page

For the next nine years, my brother and I ran a check cashing business in South Florida. My first five out had me under supervisory release, allowing my parole officers to barge in anytime unannounced. They were barely legal drinking age, so I gave them a break and barely winced or whined during drug screenings. I even passed some of Anita's wafers (the crumbling ones) onto them.

Not all of my post-pen friends made life cookies and milk. My first flame out of the cooler was nuttier than my brig bud, Crazy Eddie. I called it quits with Terry at the end of my first summer out, but she stuck to me like rancid honey. Six months later, when Donna, a carrot top from Tampa and I were smooching under the holiday mistletoe, my doorbell rang. That bell tolled for me.

Tenacious Terry showing up unannounced on New Year's Eve was a recipe for trouble, so I let her in for a few, thinking she'd simmer down and leave. After hogging the hard-to-find Hopjes Coffee Candies my brother bought me, she got amped up and told my date she was "canoodling with a con." The latching, parasitic shrub died on the spot (the mistletoe, not Terry). I double locked the door behind Donna after she bolted, then hustled a profane, proud Terry outside.

I was groggy on New Year's morning, so when I saw "FELON" scribed in serial killer-esque brown letters across my living room window, I hoped I was just hung over. Did that deranged potty-mouth use poop to smear me? I poked my head outside, and discovered red and green Hershey Kisses wrappers lying used and guilty on the ground. Sweet Jesus, that nut grinded her axe and wrote me off in Christmas chocolates.

I pitched the single apple that was my breakfast across the room, slumped into my second-hand sofa, and slept until dinner. That night I tore down the holiday lights, threw them in the garbage and turned on the news. The anchor was interviewing a new singer, Brad Paisley, who suggested New Year's Day was like, "the first blank page of a 365-page book".

A crackpot, lemonade-out-of-lemons idea hit me that could decamp the last ten years. It meant limiting my newfound free time, and undergoing another decade-long obstacle, but writing my memoir was one of the smartest ideas I ever cooked up. The book helped me examine my old self in a new world, neither of which I understood very well.

It's doubtful you'd ever want a Mafia hitman as a roommate, or a how-to on crafting candy cane shanks, but it might be delish to press your nose against the window of my life as the Otisville cook. The proof is in the pudding.

RECIPE: CHICKEN CANOODLE SOUP

    2 cans drained sweet peas
    2 cans drained corn
    2 large containers of chicken broth
    1 clove mashed garlic
    1 bag carrots
    1 pound tricolor pasta
    Olive oil

Add olive oil to a soup pot and begin to brown the garlic. Avoid the stalkings – use just the garlic bulbs. Chop and add the carrots – sans carrot tops – and cook on medium heat. Invite in the corn, peas, and chicken broth. Simmer for 30 minutes, without letting soup come to a boil. Add pasta and cook until al dente. The dish will take off, if you sprinkle in Parmesan cheese. Fills up 3 guests. *Optional*: enjoy with Terry's Ridged Potato Chips.

NEWS PAIRING: Texas' 130-year-old Moody Church had widespread damage after ransacking vandals stole chocolate from the parish kitchen and defaced the sanctuary.

"FOR YOUR LAST MEAL, DON'T ORDER CHINESE.
YOU'LL BE HUNGRY AGAIN IN AN HOUR."

PART 7

FOOD & CRIME: A LA CARTE

CHAPTER 49

THE FUSION OF FOOD & FRAUD: THE AGROMAFIA

The longest-running federal case in American history blends the Sicilian Mafia with American pizzerias. In 1984, thirty-seven Italian mobsters were indicted in "The Pizza Connection" for distributing heroin and other drugs inside tomato cans en route to US pizza parlors. The prosecutor, Rudy Giuliani, estimated that over a billion dollars worth of opiates were delivered in less than ten years. The trial lasted twenty-four months, cost $50 million and involved the FBI, DEA, US Customs, Swiss authorities, Italian national police, and the NYPD.

The "AgroMafia" targets Italy's agricultural sector, and has grown into a $16 billion a year criminal business. Profits from food-oriented injustices are triple the earnings of cocaine-related crimes. The hit list focuses primarily on wine, olive oil, and cheese; mozzarella is bleached and whitened to appear fresh, and cheap wines are repackaged as expensive clarets. Deodorizing rotten seafood is also a fishy but popular practice. In 2017, ten European countries investigated tuna illegally treated with nitrates.

Seven thousand tons of phony extra virgin olive oil was intercepted on the way to American stores in 2016. This supports the statistic that 75% stateside is not the real deal. First-pressed, extra virgin olive oil is defiled after being diluted with canola or saffron oil, and chlorophyll is added for its greenish color. In 1981, a batch of altered industrial rapeseed was sold as olive oil to street traders across Spain. Over 1,000 people died from a violent allergic reaction termed Toxic Oil Syndrome. The incident became the deadliest foodborne illness disaster in modern history.

In an interview with *The New Yorker*, Tom Mueller, author of *Extra Virginity: The Sublime and Scandalous World of Olive Oil* claims, "The earliest written mention of olive oil, on cuneiform tablets at Ebla in the twenty-fourth century B.C., describes teams of inspectors who toured olive mills on behalf of the king, looking for fraudulent practices…certain emperors rose to power on olive-oil wealth."

The intentional adulteration of food for economic gain has become a searing international problem, with the cost to the industry estimated at $15 billion a year. The chain runs from the farm door to the supermarket floor. The Italian FBI has snatched 3,500 acres of olive fields from the Mafia and returned the land to local growers. (In *The Godfather*, the Corleone family starts out in America running an olive oil company.) Italian cropper Nicola Clemenza, who hand combs olives from his trees, led two hundred farmers in a revolt against Mafia control. In retaliation, gangsters set fire to his home while his family dined at the dinner table.

Forgeries of fare so tarnish the Boot's soul and reputation for fine cuisine that the Italian government created an FBI-oriented team of culinary testers. Their findings are now considered fact in Italian law. China, Canada, England, and Scotland immediately followed with their own cookery crime units. By 2013, The US Food Standards Agency learned of 1,500 cases of top shelf trickery. The countries most vulnerable to food fraud, in order, are Italy, Spain, Pakistan, France, and India. Mislabeling, artificial enhancement, and substitution are the top shams. The most crime is committed against fish, then meat, wine, and lastly, spices.

England made headlines with the Horsemeat Scandal. Police discovered mustang meat was subbed for beef when burgers in the British Isles tested positive for equine DNA. Bangladesh firms have used formalin, used to preserve human corpses, to plump up apple sales. The head of

Ireland's largest fruit and vegetable company was jailed for six years after labeling 1,000 tons of garlic imported from China as lower-taxed fruit.

Stewart Parnell, former CEO of the Peanut Corporation of America, knowingly shipped salmonella-contaminated peanut butter across the country, killing seven people. His sentencing marked the first federal conviction in US history associated with food safety. American wholesomeness took another fall when Kraft Mac & Cheese was found to contain Yellow #5 and Yellow #6, dyes made with lice-killing coal tar.

From lice to rice: twenty-two tons of long-grain rice, sold as pricey Basmati, was seized as part of a sweep powered by Interpol and Europol. Food folly has become an art form: 85,000 pounds of spoiled olives were "renewed" when gangsters painted them with copper sulfate to make them appear young, bright and green. One of the most tasteless recalls in history was the 2005 Sudan Red Scandal. Unsavory men in India colored chili peppers with synthetically-produced, red carcinogenic dye, most used to treat leather, to produce a cheap saffron substitute.

CHAPTER 50
THE GRAPES OF WRATH

Fine wine collecting is a passion that drowns out reason or logic. Collectors love the cultured beverage, and are heavily influenced by the beauty and appearance of the bottle. Yet experts estimate that twenty percent are counterfeit.

One historic wine forgery involves the eighteenth century "Thomas Jefferson bottles". First sold via Christie's London in 1985, the decanters were purchased by Christopher Forbes for $156,000 as a gift for his father, Malcolm Forbes. They were thought to have come from a collection of wines with the initials "THJ," suggesting the investments were property of President Thomas Jefferson.

Other serious collectors sought out the famous flasks. Energy tycoon William Koch purchased five bottles for nearly $500,000. The rarities were put up for auction by twenty-five-year-old Rudy Kurniawan, who stained his career with a decade-long jail sentence for selling approximately $150 million worth of fake wines.

Winemaker Opus One implemented a security system using a chip between cork and seal which changes color when scanned for authenticity. A bottle of Gorgana white wine, harvested by convicts at Gorgana Island Prison, off the coast of Tuscany, sells for about $100 in the United States. The most famous inmate is Benedetto Ceraulo, murderer of fashion mogul Maurizio Gucci.

Grapes have a seedy past: Elizabeth Stride, Jack the Ripper's third victim, was found dead in 1888 with the fleshy berries in hand. It is believed that the notorious killer used the then-luxury fruit to lure the unlucky prostitute.

CHAPTER 51
THE GARDEN OF EATIN'

Nelson Mandela stated in his book *A Prisoner in the Garden* that, "to plant a seed, watch it grow, to tend it and then harvest it, offered a simple but enduring satisfaction". Yet it was inedible meals, high medical costs, and low budgets that led to the advent of the prison garden. What began as forced labor grew into community projects that boosted motivation and reduced inmate angst. Homegrown food became the closest cons could get to home cooking. (*Greenfingers* is a film based on the true story of convicts who till their way to stardom.)

Two acres of notoriously violent Rikers Island was transformed into the country's first penitentiary garden and greenhouse in 1997. Potatoes, cucumbers, pepper plants, and tomatoes were sold to local high-end restaurants and donated to nearby soup kitchens. The Horticultural Society of New York, and the Department of Corrections, oversee 500 inmates who cultivate the grounds year-round. The program has proven that landscaping in lockup reduces recidivism up to forty percent.

One gated garden in Missouri produced 163 tons of extra fruit and vegetables to donate to shelters, churches, and nursing homes; California cons processed three million eggs from 160,000 hens (that also live their lives out in cages). Ohio food banks suffered when ten of their jailhouse farms closed and 800,000 pounds of carrots, collard greens, beets, and cabbage were lost.

An Illinois county jail installed a large "earth tub" and began turning wasted rations into useful, organic compost. Planting Justice, a grassroots organization that empowers incarcerated people, often hires graduates from their San Quentin planting program. Chicago's Botanical Garden Program offers a one-year course for nonviolent offenders to go on 'Garden Duty' and learn horticulture, hoping a paycheck and the therapeutic powers of tilling the earth prove rehabilitative.

Inmates who work the land peacefully improve in body, mind, and spirit. But the scene can turn thorny. Felons have tried to murder each other with bloodthirsty recipes like "Toxic Tomato Plant Tea." One British inmate tried to pass a marijuana bush off as an "aromatic vegetable plant."

Is there more than a biblical link between cultivation and corruption? In the last days of his life, Osama Bin Laden took daily walks through his personal vegetable patch.

CHAPTER 52

MAD AS A WET HEN

From Eve's apple and The Boston Tea Party, to Snow White's poison apple and the Ben & Jerry's ice cream that milked its way through the O. J. Simpson trial, food and crime have been fused together since the beginning of time.

In 1626, statesman Sir Francis Bacon demanded his horse-drawn carriage be stopped, so he could pay a farm woman to slaughter and pluck a hen on the frozen London day. When she finished, Bacon stuffed the bird full of snow with his bare hands to prove that ice, rather than salt, could preserve meat. The experiment with refrigeration caused the philosopher to fall seriously ill.

Bacon was taken by the king's physician to the Earl of Arundel's home in nearby Highgate. The sixty-five-year-old soon contracted pneumonia and died. Modern poet, Pip Wilson, commemorated his death with a pitiless poem:

Against cold meats was he insured?
For frozen chickens he procured—
brought on the illness he endured,
and never was this Bacon cured.

Pond Square, believed to be the site of Bacon's dogged research, has developed a reputation for being haunted by a confused phantom chicken. In December 1943, Airman Terence Long, crossing the pond, was stunned to see a half-plucked shivering fowl. A Highgate resident confirmed seeing a ghostly "large whitish bird" again during World War II. Twenty years later, a motorist witnessed a half-plucked chicken running in circles and vanishing into thin air. In 1970, the fowl ghost interrupted a couple kissing, again circling and disappearing. Ghostly birds may not be criminal, but they do fit into the strange stories that encircle cuisine.

During World War II, twenty-five-year-old Polish secretary, Margot Woelk, was taken against her will and became one of Adolf Hitler's fifteen taste testers. The tyrant's paranoia of being poisoned by the British forced Woelk and the other fourteen women to risk their lives every day, sampling vegetarian fare before it reached the Führer's wartime bunker. Woelk recalled, "The food was delicious, only the best vegetables, asparagus, bell peppers, and always a side of rice or pasta."

Soviet troops took the heavily guarded lair a year later. They executed every food tester, except Margot Woelk. At age ninety-five, the secretary told her salacious story to the world, remembering that she cried after every meal, waiting to see if she'd live or die.

CHAPTER 53

OUTLAWED

A prison cook is hard-pressed to squeeze garlic out of any Kitchen Cop. The iconic scene from *Goodfellas,* where mob boss Paulie Cicero finely slices garlic with his razor blade, is a cinematic setup. Is it banned because it can cause poisoning, or interfere with medication? Could just extreme garlic breath, body odor, or gas cause pen riots?

Garlic slows down reaction time, which is why pilots are banned from ingesting it before flying. The inexpensive, organic cure can cause dizziness and increase the risk of excess bleeding. Now classified as hallucinogenic, Queen Elizabeth II gave the root the royal boot from Buckingham Palace.

Chinese jails use forced labor to export twenty million tons of peeled garlic a year. Prisoners are forced to peel bulbs with their teeth to avoid beatings for unfinished work. In the process, acids from the vegetable burn through their skin and melt their fingernails. Buying any food produced in this inhumane manner is now illegal in the United States.

Some bans make sense. When cooked improperly, Japanese Fugu, or puffer fish, contains enough poison to kill thirty people in twenty minutes. The sodium-blocking poison paralyzes the muscles of the fully-conscious victim, who then dies from asphyxiation. Japanese chefs train for more than three years to perfect the thirty steps needed to safely cook the exotic dish; this includes removing the still beating heart, and disposing of toxic, internal organs as if they were radioactive waste.

Food restrictions can be political. McDonald's cannot open in North Korea due to sanctions, despite the rumor that its leader has used the state airline to sneak in the famous burgers. Some bans are sanitary in nature: Austria prohibits the fat substitute Olestra, as it causes anal leakage. Restraints can be based on religion and culture: Somalia bans samosas because they resemble the Holy Trinity, and children in French schools cannot use ketchup due to its "commonness."

Some bans stink: in Southeast Asia, thou shalt not eat the fleshy, custard-like delicacy, Durian. The spiky, football-sized fruit's repulsive odor comes from sulfur compounds found in the skin. Odor comparisons have been made to dirty socks, rotting meat, dead cats, skunk, and molded cheese. Chef Anthony Bourdain warned that the tropical fruit will leave you with breath that smells "as if you'd been French-kissing your dead grandmother." Still, Durian was added to Pizza Hut's list of toppings in China in 2019, and McDonald's in Singapore started offering a Durian McFlurry shake. The following American food bans are nutty at best:

Alabama: carrying an ice cream cone in your back pocket creates a sticky legal situation.

Alaska: get a cold shoulder from the cops if you offer alcoholic drinks to a moose.

Colorado: no drinking before riding a horse, considered here a non-motorized vehicle.

Florida: hot dog vendors cannot wear a thong bikini, as public reaction poses a traffic hazard.

Idaho: things get heavy if a box of candy for your lover weighs less than fifty pounds.

Indiana: ride a streetcar within four hours of eating garlic and you'll be racing from the law.

Louisiana: it's illegal to order a pizza for an unsuspecting, ungrateful friend.

Maryland: eating while swimming in the ocean is an idea that's all wet.

Massachusetts: mourners cannot nosh on more than three sandwiches at any wake.

New Hampshire: throw a picnic in a cemetery and get a real life ticket.

New Jersey: slurping soup in The Diner Capital of the World doesn't go down well.

New Mexico: carrying a lunchbox is not a Rio Grande idea.

North Dakota: serving beer with pretzels in public creates legal buzz.

Ohio: Columbus stores may not actively sell Corn Flakes on the day of rest.

Oklahoma: taking a bite from someone's hamburger starts a tornado of trouble.

South Dakota: residents will wake to a ticket if they fall asleep in a cheese factory.

Texas: milk someone else's cow and be branded a dairy thief.

Utah: not drinking milk here is both cowardly and illicit.

Wisconsin: serving apple pie without cheese on top is criminal.

CHAPTER 54

EAT, DRINK, AND BE SCARY

Nutrition expert Dr. Joel Fuhrman stated that "America has weapons of mass destruction on every street corner. They're called donuts, cheese-burgers, potato chips." Hard to dispute, with meal items like Arby's Meat Mountain Sandwich's 44% fat content. The mound piles on chicken ten-ders, fish fillet, roast turkey, ham, corned beef, brisket, steak, roast beef, and bacon. Swiss and cheddar cheese top the mile high club.

Obesity. A hate crime against oneself? This disease kills more than 2.8 million adults a year, 300,000 in America alone. The world's fattest man, John Brower Minnoch, died at age thirty-seven weighing 1,400 pounds. He was the biggest primate to have ever lived. China's Gigantopithecus ape – a fruit eater – came close at 1000 pounds, but has been extinct for 100,000 years.

"Super Morbid Obesity" is now a medical term used to describe people with so much body fat, they are at risk of death. One documented case of obesity-related diabetes was so horrendous that the patient's legs became necrotic, leading to hundreds of maggots eating away at the dying flesh.

Sweden's King Adolf Frederick ate himself to death in 1771 after a merrymaking spread of lobster, caviar, sauerkraut, kippers, champagne, and éclairs; Henry I, King of England, expired after eating an excess of eel-like lamprey fish. Alexander the Great is known to have died after indulging in back-to-back feasts.

Sugar dependency sifted into the US legal system in 1979 as a strategy to save Dan White, the killer of gay San Francisco politician, Harvey Milk. "The Twinkie Defense" was used, filling jurors up with the notion that an overabundance of sugar, specifically binging on Hostess Twinkies, can cause deeply irrational thoughts. The golden sponge cake cover creamed its skeptics, and Dan White sat in the slammer for only seven years.

CHAPTER 55

MCRAGE

The National Employment Law Project counted more than 700 violent incidents in three years at McDonald's, seventy-two percent involving guns. In 2019, golden arches workers filed a lawsuit, alleging the company failed to protect its Chicago employees from a daily risk of violence. These fiascos are so widespread that McMurder.com tallies killings at McDonald's since 1980.

Fast food outlets suffer twice the assaults of full service establishments. (Targeting American culture, director Spike Jonze's music video *The Suburbs* plays out this scenario.) Chain restaurants are vulnerable to robbery for reasons beyond attracting the drunk, rowdy, and impatient. Drive-thrus offer hasty getaways, and cash-heavy franchises hire teenagers and close late, an unsafe combination. The following trio of fast food killings quickly made headlines across the globe:

The Burger Chef Murders. Indiana, 1978. Four Burger Chef employees were kidnapped and murdered after $581 was stolen from the restaurant safe. Thought to be a case of teen workers embezzling and running rogue, the greasy spoon was cleaned and reopened the next day, eliminating any evidence. The victims were still wearing their spirited blue and white Burger Chef uniforms when they were found dead days later in a nearby county. Forty years later, police hoped to solve the slayings by releasing a photo of the murder weapon's handle.

The Brown's Chicken Massacre. Illinois, 1993. Two robbers butchered seven Brown's Chicken staff members, tying their corpses up inside the walk-in freezer. A prime suspect was sent home by police after a frenzied, videotaped confession where he first placed himself in front of the suburban restaurant during the crime, then insisting he was inside purchasing food, and finally claiming to have killed two of the victims in the kitchen cooler. The crime was solved nine years later when police matched one suspect's DNA to saliva on partially eaten chicken found in the garbage at the crime scene.

The Fast Food Killer. Tennessee, 1997. Dennis Paul Reid Jr., a dishwasher at Shoney's restaurant in Nashville, robbed three restaurants in total and murdered seven workers. On parole at the time for holding up a steakhouse, Reid forced two Captain D's employees into the restaurant's refrigerator where he executed them. He killed three servers a month later in a Tennessee McDonald's, and later persuaded Baskin Robbins employees to let him inside for ice cream after closing. Two teenage staffers were found the next day, throats slashed, in a nearby park. Reid received seven death sentences.

The prior stories made history, but the following fast food crimes are truly bizarre:

A woman was arrested for selling a side of sexual favors with sweets at a New Jersey Dunkin Donuts; as a Taco Bell patron had an aneurysm, an employee stole her wedding ring; a Pennsylvania McDonald's server sold heroin inside Happy Meals, and three Memphis drag queens sent a McDonald's manager to the hospital after beating him with a "Caution: Wet Floor" sign. The madness of these crimes came to a head when a homeless woman offered to trade fellatio for McNuggets in the parking lot of a L.A. McDonald's.

Robbers of a French McDonald's got eaten alive by eleven patrons who were anti-terror agents; a Washington mother tried to sell her three-month-old baby at Taco Bell for $500; a man broke into a Florida Wendy's and stole the safe after cooking himself a burger, while another Floridian bribed a McDonald's cashier with drugs as payment for cheeseburgers.

An Oregon man beat his girlfriend with a cane after she failed to return home with In-N-Out; a southern belle threatened to shoot up a South Carolina Burger King because her cinnamon roll was stale, and an

Angeleno pepper sprayed a Del Taco manager because he denied her free burritos. A Wendy's worker steered child pornography to Texas patrons via the eatery's drive-thru, and lastly, a Californian stole cow costumes from Chick-Fil-A to utterly milk people on Craigslist, selling them for $350 each.

The restaurant burns the patron in these fast food fiascos:

When a woman complained of a dead fly in her yogurt, the shop owner demanded a fly autopsy to prove the insect was dead in the pint before it was opened; Subway's promise to "cut out the fat" was taken literally when a four-inch serrated knife was baked into a New York man's sandwich; an Australian family accused pub chefs of putting feces in their Frosties as revenge for them complaining about a noisy football match.

Donuts do give you big butts: an Australian woman got smoking mad after finding a cigarette end inside her sweet roll; an impatient Waffle House customer got bashed in the head with a coffee pot by a stressed-out South Carolina waiter, and musician Kid Rock was arrested in 2007 after a clash with a Waffle House customer in Georgia.

CHAPTER 56

BAKING BAD

Nutraloaf, a meatloaf-like casserole, is known in the clink as "Lockup Loaf." Inmates can be legally punished with this "special management meal" if they throw food or use kitchen utensils to, for example, flick feces.

Rice, potatoes, beans, vegetables, cheese, and milk seem like sane ingredients. But mash these unlikely items together and chow on what reporters have described as "chewing on chalk" and "the thick, pulpy aftermath of something you dissect in biology class." The cruel gruel is dispensed inside a brown paper sack, designed to be eaten only as finger food, no utensils.

Prison detainees have filed lawsuits based on the Eighth Amendment, claiming that the serving of the "behavioral management tool" is cruel and unusual punishment. In the Washington case of Gordon v. Barnett, the District Court ruled that being assigned to eating Nutraloaf is in fact punishment, and therefore captives are entitled to a hearing before being subjected to it.

Former Arizona sheriff Joe Arpaio, infamous for forcing then-inmate and heavyweight champion Mike Tyson to wear pink underwear and socks under his prison greens, won a federal judgment in 2010 addressing the constitutionality of Nutraloaf. Cook County Sheriff Tom Dart insisted that inmates got their nutritional needs met, and he would not cater to "culinary desires."

Eastern State Penitentiary's "Food Weekend" offers paying patrons the chance to sample different state Nutraloafs while touring the abandoned jail. Guests ingest bland bricks from Arkansas, Idaho, California, and Illinois. New York sacked the Loaf in 2015, but Jewish inmates were given kosher loaves in the past.

Here are the retching recipes served in ten states:

California: golden mishmash of raw cabbage, chili powder, and wheat bread.

Delaware: this lump adds pieces of pineapple to oatmeal, rice, and cheese sauce.

Florida: a mound of spinach, dried beans, dry grits and oatmeal.

Idaho: the breakfast loaf mushes together cereal, orange juice, gelatin and toast.

Illinois: a brick of spinach, applesauce, bread crumbs, beef and beans.

Milwaukee: Biscuit mix is added to celery, chili powder, potatoes and poultry.

North Carolina: this Southern loaf combines canned black-eyed peas and turnips.

Ohio: a raunchy recipe of spaghetti, salad, coffee, green beans, and cookies.

Pennsylvania: an uncommon mixture of garbanzo beans, cabbage and oatmeal.

Vermont: non-dairy cheese and canned carrots turn the raisin-rich loaf orange.

CHAPTER 57

ROTTEN TO THE CORE

The food fed to the 2.2 million incarcerated Americans is not regulated by the FDA. The warden decides who eats, and how often. In the film *Brubaker*, prison provisions serve as an example of true torture. *Brubaker* again hits the bullseye, showing a side of beef being diverted from jail and sold for personal gain to a local diner. Realistic, considering Alabama Sheriff Greg Bartlett filled up his own pockets – and was jailed – for embezzling almost $250,000 allocated for county inmate meals.

A jailed Georgian resorted to a diet of toothpaste and toilet paper when undersized portions of food were rationed by a contracted private company. Many of these outside food providers have been fined for atrocities like maggots in meals and rodent mucus on desserts. Life imitated art when a Pakistani man, guilty of killing his wife for serving lentils instead of goat meat, begged for the death sentence to avoid eating state food for life. O. J. Simpson reportedly gave coop cookery "two thumbs up," despite being classified as a "K-10" prisoner, or someone ordered to eat alone.

Though jailers in the 1800s placed lobster on internment menus, at the time considered low-class fare, it's hard to imagine keeping slammer slop down from these rotting jails:

Bang Kwang in Thailand, or "Big Tiger." Nicknamed because it eats those on the inside, famished men often catch protein-rich worms and rats to survive. Though fish head soup has been served, one bowl of dirty rice broth a day leads leg-cuffed captives into starvation. A Big

Tiger internee may get lucky and work for a wealthy con to afford goods from the on-site store. American Angela Carnegie recalls her meals here were commonly seasoned with insect larva.

Hoeryong Concentration Camp in North Korea, or "Camp 22." Two thousand people a year die from malnutrition in the former hellhole, famous for experimenting on prisoners with poisoned foodstuff. Anything edible is fair game; it is common practice to fish noodles out of "garbage ponds." Humans are kept on the verge of starvation to succumb to rewards for snitching on cellmates.

Gitarama Central in Rwanda, or "Hell on Earth." Food is so scarce that inmates are led by their primal instincts to kill and cook each other. Seven thousand rot in a space set up for four hundred. Running water is rarely found in this roofless brick box, built on the ridge of a banana commune. While men stir oil drums of beans and maize over cooking fires, people often die, burn, or choke from the smoke and fumes.

Rikers Island in New York, or "The Oven." In 2016, a man sued Rikers for eighty million dollars, claiming the food at "Torture Island" was a death sentence that caused his stomach to separate from his intestines. Ten years earlier, nineteen inmates sued New York City after blue and green-speckled meatloaf, cabbage, and corn were found to contain rat poison. Rapper Foxy Brown had guards deliver meals to her "oven" door, while other inmates have just four minutes to consume their chow. This is assuming anyone has an appetite, with nearby landfills reportedly smelling like rotten eggs due to trash-emitting, poisonous methane gas.

CHAPTER 58

COOKED

Marlon Brando runs an illicit dinner club in *The Freshman*, where endangered species like the Komodo dragon become din din for $1M. People continue to eat at-risk animals all over the world, justifying the practice as cultural.

China's most sought-after delicacies are pangolin, monitor lizards, giant salamanders, and owls. The Huanan Seafood Market in Wuhan, China was at the center of the deadly coronavirus outbreak in 2019, peddling the consumption of more than one hundred live animals, including baby crocodiles, wolf pups, foxes, rats, and peacocks. (The killing and sale of bushmeat in Africa is thought to be the source for the Ebola virus.) Hope springs with a new Chinese law forbidding the selling, buying, or eating of wild animals, protecting 400 endangered species like the giant panda.

Illegal Chinese "Tiger Feasts" have been recently exposed on social media. Smugglers deliver a tranquilized tiger by truck, and electrocute and butcher the magnificent wildcat to entertain and feed the country's political elite. The leftovers are sold on the black market, with the animal's penis hacked off for ginger tiger soup.

Dogs are not extinct, but also get slaughtered and exterminated for their flesh. Even carcasses knowingly infected with rabies are consumed in Bali. China's annual Dog Meat Festival champions eating more than 10,000 canines inside a ten-day period.

The French finch-like ortolan is a tiny, threatened bird that has been illegal to eat since 1987, yet it was sacrificed for former French President Francois Mitterrand's last meal in office. Ortolan was eaten by fatcat Bobby Axelrod on Showtime's *Billions*, representing the ultimate entrée for society's one percenters. The ortolan is trapped and blinded while flying south for the winter. The songbird is thrown in a dark box, gorged with nourishment, and then drowned in brandy. The feathers are plucked and the entire bird is roasted.

It is said Roman emperors stabbed out the eyes to make the creature think it was nightfall, and thus eat more. Custom dictates that it is chewed wearing a napkin over one's head so the aroma does not escape.

Commercial trawling for Chilean sea bass caused the fish to be nearly extinct by the end of the 1990s, yet eco-warrior Al Gore reportedly served the luxury toothfish to seventy-five guests at his daughter's Beverly Hills wedding. The owner of a trendy Santa Monica sushi restaurant, known for its exotic fare, pleaded guilty to preparing endangered sei whale meat. The fishery was fined $5,000 after two women armed with hidden cameras captured the waiter serving the delicacy for $85 a portion. Japan's mammoth supply of whale meat is now converted to lowly dog food.

CHAPTER 59

VEGETARIAN DIETS
TO DIE FOR

The vegetarian menu at Maricopa County Jail in Arizona is the first of its kind in the country. The change represents a healthier, cost-effective food program for convicts, courtesy of infamous former Arizona sheriff Joe Arpaio. Even veggie meals dished out in 2015 by Playboy playmate and animal activist Pamela Anderson couldn't stop the chaos among cons who hated the plan.

Were Arpaio's meatless meals born after green bologna sandwiches were served in 2004? Singer Glen Campbell refused them while locked up at Maricopa jail, while basketball star Charles Barkley had all his eats delivered while living outdoors in the prison's "Tent City." A peanut butter sandwich, oranges, and crackers made up brunch – breakfast and lunch combined into one cheaper course. Overcooked vegetables and soy were the Arizona dinners.

American prisoners have had a widespread affair with peanut butter and jelly for a century. A Rhode Island bar recently created a Peanut Butter & Jelly Crime Cocktail to honor the eminent fusion. (A Florida convict actually requested PB&J as his last meal before execution.) This favorite had its start as a military ration during World War II, but ironically has triggered bullpen riots.

A Michigan inmate filed a lawsuit when PB&J was substituted after breakfast waffles ran out, citing the nutty sandwiches caused riots.

A Nevada inmate sued the state when the crunchy kind replaced the smooth sort. American cons, furious over the minuscule amount of jelly once supplied, held a sit-in after being forced to eat jam-free "choke sandwiches." One California food distributor supplied twenty prisons with two million pounds of peanut butter and jelly in a single year. "Peanut butter and jelly" took its deadliest turn when the FBI deduced that the four words were terrorist code for "Jihad."

CHAPTER 60

BAD PITT

Life is a bowl of cherries, if you can manage to avoid the pits. Beware, and don't let the soft flesh, delicate aroma, and velvety skin of peaches, plums, cherries, apricots, nectarines, pears, and mangos fool you. They may taste sweet and sensual, but these deceiving stone fruits are lethal weapons.

When the pits of "drupes" are crushed, chewed, or split, they metabolize into poisonous cyanide, giving new meaning to choke cherries. Less than a dozen broken and digested cherry pits will put anybody belly up. It takes little more than a dime-sized amount of the potentially fatal chemical to kill a 150-pound person in ten minutes. It's fruitless to look for warning labels on single-seed packages; they don't exist.

Cyanide is derived from organic plant alkaloids that concentrate in the heart of peaches, apricots, and apple seeds. If a pit is swallowed whole, the toxin stays safely inside its hard hull. Shatter the shell, and unleash a crushing, oxygen-deprived death to your body's cells. Famed American toxicologist Walter Haines recounted a woman who committed suicide by intentionally gnawing on twenty peach pits.

Mangos, peruvian peppers, pistachios, and cashews are all members of the Anacardiaceae family tree. They all bear stone fruits that can contain the irritant urushiol, a potentially toxic oil if ingested. The sappy resin can also cause poison ivy-like rashes and burns.

Bitter or raw almonds are dangerous, deadly fruits. As of 2007, they are illegal to sell in the United States, as ingesting just a handful can be potentially fatal to children. It's their woody aroma one smells after a cyanide poisoning; recent studies pinpoint a genetic mutation that, through history, turned almonds from toxic to enticing.

Though they sprout off trees full of cheerful pink blossoms, bitter or raw almonds contain forty-two times more venom than nuttier-tasting sweet almonds, often found in foods like marzipan and nougat. Yet, the two brown sister fruits do look alike.

CHAPTER 61
EATING IN

American inmates can choose from more than one hundred items a week off prison commissary menus. Prisoners fill out request forms, similar to what hotel guests complete to assure breakfast will be waiting at their door in the morning. Choosing and buying commissary items is the one aspect cons have control over: it is estimated that $1.6 billion was spent in 2016; one hundred million dollars alone was spent inside Texas commissaries.

Pizza kits, Pop-Tarts and taco mix; salmon and summer sausages; mackerel and marshmallows; they all make the cut. Vanilla cappuccino, cream cheese, pork rinds and pudding also make the grade. Baby octopus for a dollar, oysters for two dollars, and squeeze-cheese for three; these varying items are affordable and appear on most commissary lists, unless you pull a Charles Manson and get your spending limit slashed for dealing drugs in the can.

Scott Peterson's San Quentin food list revealed the convicted killer ordered up smoked scallops, oysters, garlic sauce, and granola. When John Gotti's commissary list was sold at auction in 2010, it was uncovered that the New York mob boss – with a spending limit of $37.50 a week – had a grave addiction to sweets, specifically, Three Musketeers bars, Snickers, and pure sugar cubes. (Sugary Jolly Ranchers candies have been melted down in jail to be used as hair gel.)

Casey Anthony had "donors" who padded her canteen account pre-acquittal. This allowed her to earnestly enjoy cocoa butter and cheese puffs. Murderer Jodi Arias cooked up a less-than-seductive list of sardines, clams, and gas-reducing Beano.

Martha Stewart concocted her famous Crab Apple Jelly behind bars. She took the heat for illegally pulling the fruit from on-site branches outside her West Virginia jail, which is nicknamed "Camp Cupcake." (Stewart told reporters she "really missed lemons" after she was put on ice.) She also made news for getting caught smuggling brown sugar and cinnamon back to her cell. (Disgruntled inmates told the media she hid them inside her bra.) According to *People* magazine, Martha Stewart and twenty-five female prison pals held a potluck dinner before her release; North Carolina's (now-imprisoned) agricultural commissioner supplied the pineapple cheesecake.

O. J. Simpson blew up to 300 pounds in the brig and was, by all accounts, addicted to coop chow. Former linebacker Ray Lewis sustained himself on oranges for the first week of his sentence, to avoid moldy slammer slop. Lindsay Lohan did fourteen days in solitary, but was allowed to order out. Oscar Pistorius reportedly lives on chakalaka in jail, a canned vegetable relish, to avoid being poisoned in the pen (officials allow him to cook his own meals).

Peanut butter and hot sauce mixed into ramen makes up perfect Pokey Pad Thai. Ramen noodles are top shelf currency, but are bland when served "butt naked," or without sauce. Inmates have mated jelly with ketchup to conceive sweet and sour sauce, while big house "Le Jus Teriyaki" is the coming together of strawberry jelly and soy sauce. Parole Day Cheesecake, a recipe from the book *Prison Ramen*, slams together nuked vanilla creamer, cream cheese, Sweet'N Low, powdered Kool-Aid and cookies. Offbeat, like Rapper Lil' Kim's claim that fellow prisoners in Federal pen made her a killer, triple-layer Oreo cake.

Kool-Aid has its own page in prison food history. One penitentiary recipe for "Hard Time Candy" calls for working the flavored powder into a lump while adding hot sauce. Female prisoners often eat the dry powder like a Pixie Stick, and Kool-Aid mixed with sugar is known as "Happy Crack." The orange flavor can be mixed as a syrup with pork and rice to pump up the rind.

If you have a sadistic need to eat inside a slammer, head to China and lockdown a reservation at The Jail, where diners are fingerprinted and handcuffed inside simulated cells. Or sentence yourself to a seat at In Galera, an eatery inside a working Milan lockup where the chef and head waiter are the only civilians on staff. (Book weeks in advance so you can dine under the Italian *Escape from Alcatraz* poster.)

Life in the can doesn't necessarily mean eating from the tin. Considering the fresh food once available at Alcatraz, a con's culinary experience can be downright redeeming. Here are the best foods available in a worst-cell scenario.

Eastern State Penitentiary, Philadelphia. In the 1830s, boiled salted beef was served; the 1950s catered in Salisbury steak and an on-site bakery. A live tour now offers sample menus and a history of the noted nibbles eaten throughout the pen's biting history.

Guantanamo Bay, Cuba. Detainees can choose from eight meal types, three times a day. Choices include high fiber, vegetarian, fish, or soft bland spreads, with no food choice repeated for two weeks. Entrees like breaded chicken with lemon and garlic are available. Blueberry coffee cake and chocolate chip cookies are baked fresh on site. Halal desserts are always provided.

Her Majesty's Prison Forest Bank, England. A recent exposé revealed that "fat and bulky" internees were being given five luxury meals a day, with menus offering almost one hundred meat and dessert choices. The public was outraged learning how their tax money was being eaten up.

Los Angeles County Jail, California. The "Luxury Suite" ensures VIPs won't get eaten alive by common criminals. Eighty square feet of private living space has housed the famous – Richard Pryor, Sean Penn – and the fatal, like night stalker Richard Ramirez, Hillside Strangler Kenneth Bianchi, and O. J. Simpson. All had the benefit of picnic-style lunches and beefsteak dinners.

Bastoy Prison, Norway. Considered the world's nicest jug, Bastoy sits on an island that is home to just 115 occupants. Fish balls with white sauce, prawns, chicken con carne, and salmon are served. Each inmate is allocated an $85 food budget for their incarceration-vacation. Groceries are purchased from the island mini-mall for self-cooked breakfasts.

CHAPTER 62

THE ROCK 'N ROLLS

Alcatraz is the site of the most famous prison escape in history. "The Rock" was also known for housing the bottom of the barrel butchers. Less known: these dicey men ate near gourmet grub, as the warden believed feeding inmates unlimited quality food was first-class insurance against riots.

The chow was tops, and there was plenty of it. Breakfast items like stewed peaches, hot griddle cakes, and raspberry buns were common. Entrées from the famed menu included breaded rock cod, baked meat croquettes, roast pork shoulder, chili con carne, split pea soup, boiled corned beef with cabbage, and béchamel and sage sauces. Desserts like apricot pie, bread pudding, layer cake, and iced cupcakes were regularly dished up.

Alcatraz cons were well fed, but hardly well bred. Infamous tenants include bootlegger mobster, Machine Gun Kelly; attempted escapee Henri Young, famous for his food strikes, and Al Capone, who, among other unspeakable crimes, began cornering the American milk market in the 1930s.

Some jailbirds get meaty deliveries. In 2015, prison staff member Joyce Mitchell hid hacksaw blades in frozen hamburger meat, and delivered barbecue and Big Macs to famed Clinton Correctional escapees Richard Matt and David Sweat.

CHAPTER 63

ICEBERG: LETTUCE LIVE!

The Titanic was famous for her cultured food. Sadly, a cascade of criminally immoral events led to the luxury liner serving its last supper at the bottom of the North Atlantic Sea.

Delicacies from a first class, ten-course dinner menu included oysters, grilled mutton chops, roast squab, corned ox tongue, filet mignon, duck, and foie gras. Roquefort and Camembert cheeses, custard pudding, and chocolate éclairs were served on English china. Second class passengers banqueted on baked haddock, curried chicken, spring lamb with mint sauce, puréed turnips, buckwheat cakes, wine jelly, and tartlets.

Third classers were content with rabbit pie, smoked herring, roast beef, sweet corn, currant buns, rhubarb, and marmalade, plum pudding, and stewed figs. (The flip side of third class menus doubled as postcards that would never be sent.) On the 1996 set of James Cameron's *Titanic*, eighty crew members fell ill from lobster chowder poisoned with the drug angel dust.

A Greek bidder in London bought a single Spillers & Bakers cracker salvaged from the wreck for $23,000. The biscuit was said to be part of a survival kit onboard one of the few rescue boats. Auctioneers Henry Aldridge & Son Ltd. called the relic "the world's most valuable biscuit."

First class survivor Abraham Lincoln Salomon was rescued from the water by lifeboat #1. He foresaw the infamy of the tragic sinking, tucking a tattered menu into his pocket as the ship sank. It sold for $88,000 in 2015.

CHAPTER 64

CAFFEINE CAPERS

More than two billion cups of coffee a day are consumed worldwide. With brew so much a part of life, it makes sense that the bold, brown liquid would have a few black marks against it.

Take the Coffee Murder Case of Indonesia. An innocent date at a Jakarta cafe ended with cyanide-laced iced cappuccino. More hype when an American woman was arrested and strip-searched by religious police in Saudi Arabia for drinking coffee with a male at Starbucks.

A Connecticut police dog sniffed out sixteen bags of crack cocaine, hidden in a bag of coffee grounds inside a woman's pants. A Michigan man awaited trial after his estranged spouse was found lifeless with a plate of wet espresso grounds nearby; he had tried to convince friends that coffee can cover up the smell of a corpse.

Another unhappy husband poisoned his wife's café during "a nasty divorce." The killer got just sixty days in jail, despite a hidden camera capturing him spiking her brew with drugs. One Chicago hubby proved he was bad to the last drop: he fatally shot his wife for leaving the coffee maker on.

Italian crime families are bullying restaurants into exclusively selling brews backed by mobsters. Bar and restaurant owners are usually willing to pay the higher price for fear of retribution. Con-turned-actor Danny Trejo markets and sells whole bean espresso through his company, Trejo's Coffee; *Crime & Conspiracies with Coffee, Coffee and Crime Time*, and *True Crime and Coffee Beans* are all popular podcasts that mix morning mud with murder. More macabre: Abigail Folger, heiress to the Folgers coffee fortune, was one of Charles Manson's victims.

The Netherlands gives young prisoners a chance to redeem themselves by promoting native coffee brands in a special work program; the Coffee Crafter Co. in America offers a course for cons to learn the art of gourmet grounds and earn barista certificates to help secure work upon release. Los Angeles neighborhoods are hosting "Coffee with a Detective," a forum where the public can ask questions like "Why is the temperature of a coffee pot often used as crime scene evidence?"

Starbucks has aided felons with work experience, allowing them to pack pricey Christmas brews. Coffee comes to the rescue when a group of Kansas tweens used jolting-hot java to fend off a predator.

CHAPTER 65

KILLER CHOCOLATE

Seventy percent of the earth's chocolate comes from The Ivory Coast, Cameroon, Ghana, and Nigeria. The dark side? The sweet cash crop leads to cruel child labor on many cacao farms. More than 150 years after the abolition of slavery, the bitter truth is that chocolate companies cannot guarantee slave-free products, even with chocolate being one of the world's most consumed foods.

It takes nearly 400 cocoa beans to make a single pound of chocolate, yet fairtrade chocolate represents less than 1% of the $7 billion in yearly, worldwide sales. *The Guardian* reported that workers in the industry earn about a dollar a day, while exposed to harsh heat and unhealthy pesticides.

Chocolate's profitability and euphoric allure drives people to madness and crime. Cadbury encouraged the British public in 1985 to trespass and dig on protected archeological sites in an advertising campaign known as the "Crème Egg Scandal." Chocolate's boiling point? As a heated weapon behind bars, since the cream will burn skin on contact.

The Nazi's planned to assassinate Winston Churchill with exploding candy bars. Adolf Hitler's bomb makers coated explosive devices with a thin layer of dark cocoa, packaging them as Peters Chocolates, in lavish black and gold paper. Secret agents planned to place them in the dining room used by the English War Cabinet. The plot was destroyed by a British spy who had an illustrator draw the convoluted candy so they could be easily recognized.

Christiana Edmunds, aka the Chocolate Cream Killer, laced confections with poison in the 1870s, sickening her lover's wife and sending a four-year-old to an early grave. Scottish socialite, Madeleine Smith became the subject of a sensational poisoning trial in 1857 after serving her beloved a cup of cocoa d'arsenic.

An Italian grandmother mistakenly poisoned herself, her husband, their son, and her two grandchildren after serving a too-old, toxic packet of hot chocolate. More intentional: a New York City mother who murdered her nut-allergic eight-year-old with peanut M&Ms.

Serial cannibal Jeffrey Dahmer worked the graveyard shift at the Ambrosia Chocolate Factory in Milwaukee as a mixer; a Syrian refugee stowed away in a heated tank of liquid chocolate on a truck bound for England (he had to keep his legs moving to avoid getting trapped in the cream). An enterprising American tried smuggling $1M of cocaine inside Ferrero Rocher chocolates on a return visit from Columbia.

Author Joanna Carl is famous for her series of chocoholic mystery books, while Roald Dahl's beloved *Charlie and the Chocolate Factory* uses the sweets to sift out sin. When Edvard Munch's master painting *The Scream* was stolen, the Mars Corporation, promoting its new dark chocolate M&M, offered two million pieces of the candy as a reward for the painting's return.

The Jesus Christ-themed chocolate statue, *My Sweet Lord*, was made with 200 pounds of conflict-causing cocoa. Its creation caused artist Cosimo Cavallaro to receive death threats.

CHAPTER 66

CANDY CANED

Holiday kills are hard to digest, despite Murder Mystery Dinner Theater being a top destination on New Year's Eve. Is it excess eggnog, the push to act merry, or old-fashioned money woes that cause everyone's Uncle Eddie to snap? Maybe it's mere mention of the word: Holiday, Florida has a crime rate 72% higher than the state's other cities.

Convicted double murderer Michael Lambrix, who invited his victims to his Florida home for Spaghetti dinner before doing away with them, asked, before execution, to paint Easter eggs, hang Christmas stockings on the execution table, and have his lethal injection drug be dyed green for St. Patrick's Day. In addition to asking to trick or treat in his cell block, his last meal request was a Thanksgiving dinner.

In April alone, Americans celebrate Caramel Popcorn Day, Empanada Day, National Peanut Butter and Jelly Day, Chinese Almond Cookie Day, and National Cheese Fondue Day. The Dutch celebrate New Year's Day by devouring Fried Oil Balls, while the Viennese fill up on pig-shaped sweets to start the year.

Poles choose pickled herring on the first of the year, while people from Madrid eat a grape for every toll of the midnight bell. People die every New Year's in Japan after choking on traditional steamed rice mocha, and more deaths occur on December 31 from flying champagne corks than year-round spider bites. The following crimes are unseasonable at best.

Murder on Valentine's Day is particularly heartless. A New York University professor was accused of mailing poisoned V-Day chocolates to the judge who jailed him. A Baptist minister executed his wife in 2013 on Saint Valentine's Day, leading police to believe the cold-hearted crime was a gift to his twenty-year-old sweetheart. Parents of a Parkland, Florida school shooting victim made heart-shaped candies adorned with anti-gun slogans like "don't shoot" and "he's gone" to honor their son's Feb. 14th death.

An extortion gang terrorized Tokyo by placing cyanide-laced sweets on store shelves Valentine's Eve; the packets were marked "You'll die if you eat this." Bricks broken during Chicago's 1929 St. Valentine's Day Massacre were used to build Canada's largest barbecue restaurant. On February 14, circa 270 AD, Roman priest Valentinus was beheaded for conducting secret marriage ceremonies.

A seventeen-year-old girl prepared collard greens with a side of termite killer for Grandma on Easter Sunday in 2014. The poisoning was revenge for having her cell phone confiscated. One four-year-old was left bloodied after a raging Easter egg hunt went wrong in a calm Connecticut town, and a German elder, annoyed at children stealing Easter toys from his yard, sprayed holiday chocolate bunnies with rat poison as a treat for the curious kiddies.

The 1975 "Easter Sunday Massacre" occurred inside a private home in Ohio. A mass murderer killed eleven members of his family, who had staged an Easter egg hunt on their grandmother's lawn earlier that day. One child was found by police with a chocolate Easter egg in his lifeless hand.

President Zachary Taylor enjoyed a July 4, 1850 celebration ingesting copious amounts of iced milk and cherries; he died five days later from gastroenteritis. Football star-turned-murderer Aaron Hernandez scored free Cream of Wheat and meatloaf in jail on Independence Day. An eighteen-year-old Domino's delivery girl set out on July 4, 1982 with a stack of pizzas, never to be seen again. Witnesses discovered her car near a fireworks show, with crushed Domino's Pizza boxes nearby.

Eating 1,627 Halloween candy corns can administer a lethal dose of sugar. Surely a better way to go than being poisoned by "The Candyman," a Texas dad who offed his eight-year-old son on Halloween in 1974 with cyanide-laced Pixie Sticks to get his hands on $20,000 in life insurance. Pop also gave cyanide-laced candy to his daughter and three other children, to have his son's murder appear random.

A man who attempted to rob an Illinois Subway Sandwiches in a Halloween ghost mask looked frightful after being burned with a pot of hot soup; one of the nation's top 10/31 destinations, "Terror Behind the Walls," is a tour of Eastern State Penitentiary in Philadelphia. The stockade's speakeasy serves beverages inside Al Capone's actual cell block.

Turkey Day turned murky when five Long Island teens hurled a stolen, twenty-pound frozen bird off a bridge, forcing an oncoming driver to undergo a Thanksgiving Day tracheotomy. Gobble up this real-life recipe for Fried Hand Pies: on Thanksgiving 1991, twenty-three-year-old Omaima Nelson butchered and cooked her California groom. The Egyptian model boiled and burned her husband's hands in a deep fat fryer to remove his fingerprints. Authorities found the man's head in Nelson's freezer, garnished with leftover holiday meats and sauces. The killer's neighbor recalled the garbage disposal grinding all weekend.

A New Mexico woman faced charges after stabbing a wheelchair-bound man in the eye with a plastic candy cane. Not as dangerous as a candy cane shank – eight-inches long, sharpened to a twenty degree point, which can really be bad for your holiday health. In *The House on Sorority Row*, the killer uses the sharp end of a candy cane to kill; in *Black Christmas* a sharpened candy cane wastes a prison guard. Does this sweet know no mercy? Candy canes also contain xylitol, which poisons over 6,000 dogs a year.

A wife spiked her beloved's cherry drink with antifreeze on a cold December 25th; a monstrous mom was convicted of hiring men to finish off her four-year-old during a nativity trip to eat pizza. A Florida woman, employed to buy groceries for a family friend, strangled the victim and buried her under a pile of Christmas gifts. Actor Charlie Sheen was a lot luckier: he enjoyed prime rib and Cornish hen inside his Aspen jail cell on Xmas.

Twenty years after the 1996 Christmas slaying of JonBenét Ramsey, Colorado police are unraveling why undigested pineapple found in the tot's tummy may be key to solving her murder. Patsy Ramsey had no memory of serving fruit to her child, though the bowl held the fingerprints of mom and nine-year-old son, Burke. Pineapple was not served at the party the family attended that night.

CHAPTER 67

THE LAST SUPPERS

Jesus washed his disciples' feet at The Last Supper to cleanse them of their sins, according to The Gospel of John. Though a prisoner can mercifully choose the last thing he eats before execution, you'd be hard pressed to find anyone washing a felon's foot on death row.

Granting final meal requests demonstrates the importance of food in American life and death. In Louisiana, the warden traditionally joins a condemned man for his last meal. Is the key master trying to ward off the ghost of the accused, in fear it will haunt the executioners, per medieval legend? You don't have to believe this spooky saga to find "ultimate feasts" fascinating.

Artist Giorgia Zardetto interprets final food photos of the soon-to-be executed; Ningen Restaurant in Tokyo serves famous last meals to curious customers; Texas rubbed out last meals in prison, thanks to a con who requested twenty-five items and ate zero. The wasted entrees included two chicken fried steaks, a bowl of okra, three bacon cheeseburgers, meatloaf, pizza, peanut butter fudge, and fajitas.

Florida black widow Judy Buonoano barely digested her health-conscious choice of broccoli, asparagus, and strawberries before getting the chair in 1998. Double murderer Thomas Grasso used his last breath to let Oklahoma reporters know he was denied the SpaghettiOs he requested. An Orthodox Jew awaiting execution ironically requested a ham sandwich as his last meal. Another condemned man requested indigestion tablets, jesting he might get "gas on his stomach."

Below are the last meals of the hideous, the famous and the historical:

Abraham Lincoln: presidential feast of mock turtle soup, roast fowl, and baked yams.

Adolf Hitler: cyanide chaser between courses of spaghetti and fried eggs.

Cleopatra: smooth-skinned figs with bewitching cobra poison.

Elvis Presley: six king-sized, chocolate chip cookies.

Frank Sinatra: grilled cheese prepared his way, without bits of garlic.

JFK: two boiled Dallas eggs with bacon, orange juice, toast.

James Dean: the American rebel ordered apple pie and a glass of milk.

Jesus Christ: the Bread of God took in bitter herbs, plank bone, and possibly slaughtered lamb.

Jimi Hendrix: one tuna sandwich, which he vomited up and choked on. Not cool.

Joan of Arc: a simple request of communion; ended up with a stake.

John Belushi: the comic dosed on The Rainbow Bar and Grill's famous lentil soup.

John Lennon: gave pieces of corned beef a final chance at NYC's Stage Deli.

John Wayne Gacy: a clownish meal of a pound of strawberries and a bucket of KFC.

Julia Childs: the master chef enjoyed a bowl of her own French onion soup.

Julius Caesar: took a knife to mutton chops and mussels after dictating his dinner request.

Kobe Bryant: the basketball star scored points from above: communion was his last meal.

Kurt Cobain: the singer enjoyed dark notes of root beer soda.

Liberace: less-than-showy bowl of Cream of Wheat porridge.

Mahatma Gandhi: soulful mix of goat milk, ginger, carrot, and aloe juice.

Marilyn Monroe: robust meatballs and large stuffed mushrooms with champagne.

Martin Luther King Jr.: civil meal of black-eyed peas, fried chicken, and cornbread.

Michael Jackson: thrilling mix of spinach salad and chicken breast.

Mozart: not-so-genius choice of pork cutlets keyed with worms.

Napoleon: liver, kidneys, and garlic toast that may have betrayed his stomach.

Prince: a medley of roasted red pepper bisque and kale salad.

Princess Diana: royal mix-up of mushroom omelet, Dover sole, and veggie tempura.

Queen Victoria: known for her royal appetite, the sovereign only ingested a lick of milk.

Saddam Hussein: Iraq's less-than-sweet head of state was full of hot water and honey.

Ted Bundy: took a final stab at a bloody, medium rare steak and loose eggs.

Timothy McVeigh: the bomber demolished two pints of Ben & Jerry's mint ice cream.

-END-